# The Way of Torah and the Path of Dharma

*Intersections between*
*Judaism and the Religions of India*

## Rabbi Daniel Polish

**Ben Yehuda Press**
Teaneck, New Jersey

Published by Ben Yehuda Press
122 Ayers Court #1B
Teaneck, NJ 07666
BenYehudaPress.com

To subscribe to our monthly book club and support independent Jewish publishing, visit patreon.com/BenYehudaPress

Ben Yehuda Press books may be purchased at a discount by synagogues, book clubs, and other institutions buying in bulk. For information, please email markets@BenYehudaPress.com.

Cover illustration by Siona Benjamin.

ISBN13 978-1-953829-39-9 paper

22 23 24 / 10 9 8 7 6 5 4 3 2          20231217

*Dedication*

With

Everlasting gratitude for the past
David Polish
Aviva Friedland Polish
(Proverbs 23:25)

Thankful delight in the present
Gail
(Song of Songs 4:10)
Jonathan and Sarah
Ari and Anne
Leah
(Proverbs 23:24)

Unending hope for the future
Noa
Talia
David
Zachary
Lucy
(Proverbs 17:6)

# Contents

# Contents

# Preface

I start this book and write these words as humanity is in the midst of a pandemic that has gripped the entire planet. Covid-19 has not respected political boundaries or geographic barriers. It does not discriminate along racial or religious lines. And it has taken a terrible toll—on people, on businesses, on our social support networks, and more. And yet in the midst of this darkness we see the glimmer of good. People everywhere are increasingly recognizing that we all are, in the words of a poem by Archibald MacLeish, "Riders on the earth together, brothers [and sisters] in Eternal Cold." The myriad distinctions that conventionally separate us seem less consequential right now. Perhaps—we hope—that new consciousness will persist once this common foe has been vanquished—or at least subdued.

At this moment of human solidarity, I invite you to join me in exploring an unfamiliar and too little explored corner of interfaith dialogue. The words "Behold how good," from the very beginning of Psalm 133, have become a virtual byword in gatherings of Jews and Christians, and increasingly Muslims: "Behold how good and how pleasant it is for brothers [and sisters] to come together as one." These groups are joined together by long and complicated histories. For the last two thousand years (fifteen hundred in the case of Islam) members of these communities of faith have interacted, borrowed from one another, struggled with one another, and shared the foundational belief in the Oneness of God. More recently they have taken to referring to themselves collectively as Abrahamic faiths—asserting the shared patrimony of what each of the groups refers to as "our father Abraham." Beneath their not inconsequential differences, they celebrate a common kinship.

But is it possible to have the same kind of engagement with people with whom we have not shared millennia of interaction, with whom we do not share a common "father" or even the fundamental perspective of monotheism? Can these "others" also be the "brothers [and sisters] with whom it is good and pleasant to come together as one?" A relatively small number of Jews have explored aspects of the religious traditions of India. It is commonplace for young Israelis, upon completion of their military obligation, to go trekking in India, and likely find themselves exposed to the religious traditions of that subcontinent. Some in the Jewish community find these engagements with India to be disturbing, somehow threatening, to the welfare of the Jewish people. And yet, if good can come of our engagement with the other Abrahamic traditions, why can we not benefit from encounters with those who live outside the tent of Abraham? This book grows from my belief that Jews can gain a lot—even learn much about our own Jewish tradition—by seeing Judaism in the context of traditions ostensibly quite different from our own.

I write from the perspective of a committed Jew, one who revels in the traditions of my people, whose life is given meaning and beauty by the perspectives and practices of Jewish thought and life, and who has been moved by the richness of the religious lives of people of other traditions. And rather unexpectedly I have been—as I hope you will be—enriched by the opportunity to see Jewish tradition more clearly in the reflected light of the very different traditions of India. There have been times when I understood things about Jewish life that would not have occurred to me had I not encountered something in another tradition that revealed to me something about my own. This book will share some of these experiences with you.

# Introduction

There have been Jewish communities in India for thousands of years. And yet, it seems that Indian Jews didn't adapt any Indian religious patterns, nor did the Indian Jewish presence have any lasting effect on Indian religious practice. Today there are hardly any Jews at all left in India, most of them having long ago emigrated to the State of Israel. But it is somewhat striking that there was much less interaction between Indian and Jewish traditions in India than there historically has been with the other two Abrahamic traditions.

Of course, it makes sense to talk about the relationship of the Jewish and Christian traditions. It is commonly accepted that the Christian tradition emerged out of second Temple Judaism. The story of the subsequent relationship was dark and tragic. But it was also intense. Jews and Christians continued to live in proximity to one another. And the intellectual leaders of the two traditions continued to be aware of the other, and each tradition, in its own way, appropriated from the other. Later, Islam would emerge from the Arabian Peninsula with a profound awareness of, and indebtedness to, the two predecessor traditions. Jewish, Christian, and Muslim traditions continue to exert an influence on one another. Indeed, it is almost impossible to study any of them without reference to the others.

Whenever we encounter similarities in some aspect of any of the Abrahamic traditions, the logical approach is to explore the way they have borrowed from one another or influenced one another. Resemblances of ideas or practices among them are family resemblances. The explanations of them most likely will be found through historical investigation. An encounter with the traditions of India will involve a different set of perspectives.

The striking thing—and I would argue the useful thing—about looking at the Jewish tradition and the traditions of India in relation to one another is precisely the fact that there was largely no interaction between them. Whatever similarities there might be, then, are not the result of influence in one direction or the other. Similar religious elements are not the result of borrowing or imitation. As a result, they may say something about the very nature of human religiousness.

The Hindu tradition, in particular, offers a parallel to the Jewish tradition unlike any other in the world. Both are what we could call "root" traditions. Each seems to have come into the world without a clearly defined predecessor. Both were initially as tied to a particular location as any tribal society—a subject to which we will return in one of the later chapters. And both became "mother" traditions; Israel giving birth first to the Christian tradition and then Islam; the Hindu tradition yielding the Jain, Buddhist, and Sikh traditions. How each relates to its daughter traditions is the subject of historical analysis. But before the birth of those subsequent traditions, each represents a fresh expression of its own unique ideas and practices. In this regard the similarities they share stand outside the realm of history—they cannot be attributed to their interaction with each other—but may be seen as the result of a pure human religiosity expressing itself. As such, what they share may give us a richer understanding of the phenomenon of religion itself.

For Jews, the experience of looking at elements of these two root traditions offers another opportunity. As with anything that we have known our whole lives, it is possible to become so familiar with aspects of Jewish tradition that we simply take them for granted, lose awareness of their contours. Someone has compared such familiarity with that of a fish to water. You cannot ask a fish to describe water. And for many Jews, our religious rituals and practices can be so familiar that we hardly see them anymore. So the chance to see them in an unfamiliar light might throw their contours into new relief—enable us to see them more fully, perhaps make them more vivid and fresh for us.

## A Word About Methodology

One lens we will use in discussing Jewish and Indian traditions is the phenomenology of religion: much less complicated or fearsome than its cumbersome name suggests. The phenomenology of religion involves looking at an idea, ritual, or practice that is similar among various traditions and exploring its structure and underlying meaning independent of the manifest content, the theological, historical or ideological meanings associated with it in the traditions involved. It is a comparison of religious phenomena: not for the purpose of asserting or implying the superiority of one or another, but of looking for the underlying, innermost meaning that is at the heart of all the various expressions of that phenomenon. Through it, we can become aware of all the subtle, implicit contents of that idea, ritual, or practice, in all of the traditions in which it appears.

A good example of this is the relationship of Easter and Passover in the Christian and Jewish traditions. We are all familiar with the various historical associations. The New Testament goes out of its way to situate the trial, crucifixion, and resurrection of Jesus during Passover. And in the millennia that followed, the two holidays were also often, tragically, conjoined. The arrival of Passover evoked accusations against Jews of using the blood of Christian children in their matzah; just as the arrival of Easter, itself, aroused dread in Jewish communities, as the telling of the Passion story could move pious Christians to launch attacks against the "perfidious Jews" close at hand.

Within each tradition the holidays have very specific meanings—meanings quite different from each other. But in looking phenomenologically, our attention is drawn to the not incidental fact that both holidays take place during the spring, the time that the earth returns from the captivity and death associated with winter. This cannot be accidental or inconsequential. Indeed, it might be a dimension of each of the holidays that we would, otherwise, not accord appropriate significance. For our earlier ancestors, winter was a time of seclusion and dread. The oppression of long periods of darkness, and the anxiety of food scarcity—winter being a time of no harvest and dependence on there being enough food stored away in the fall—must have made the end of that season an occasion of great release and relief. Both holidays celebrate, each in its own way, rebirth: the return to life. Each holiday expresses this theme in its own vocabulary, using its own symbols, and referring to its basis in its own historical roots. But looking at one of the holidays in the light of the other throws the underlying theme—and its relation to the natural world—into sharper relief than would be evident by looking at either in isolation.

The issue of influence and borrowing looms large when discussing similarities between any of the Abrahamic traditions. But when we look at elements (phenomena) of the traditions of Israel and India, where the likelihood of interaction is very small, we have a rich opportunity to encounter religious expressions that have not been shaped by one tradition's influence of on the other. In this way, these traditions offer a more fertile field for phenomenological examination than the more familiar comparisons among the Abrahamic traditions.

## A Brief Discussion of
## the Long History of Indian Religion

The earliest recorded texts of Indian religion we have are the Vedas, which are usually dated around 1200 BCE. They focus primarily on a variety of sacrifices and the priests who officiated at them. These sacrifices were considered essential for maintaining harmonious relations between human beings and the many gods. The gods themselves seem to be embodiments of various elements of nature, such as the sun, thunderstorms, fire, various animals, and more.

In time, the religious patterns described in the Vedas gave way to new forms of religious expression. In the eight century BCE, a layer of commentative texts on the Vedas, called Vedanta (end of the Vedas) or Upanishads, essentially treated the sacrifices and the gods of the earlier texts as allegorical lessons about what in the West is called Pantheism: the fundamental unity of all existence, the recognition that all things are one.

In the sixth century BCE two great religious figures drastically reformulated the traditional religious patterns. Gautama the Buddha and Mahavira introduced ideas and patterns that would become the Buddhist and Jain traditions respectively. Though we tend to identify the Buddhist tradition with China, Japan, and Asia more generally, it is important to remember that its origins and presuppositions are Indian. Though the Buddhist tradition significantly diminished in India, the Jain tradition continues to be a significant part of the Indian religious landscape.

Somewhat later, from 500 BCE onward, the constellation of religious ideas and practices to which we have attached the name Hinduism became the dominant form of religious expression in India, and is the form of that tradition with which we are currently familiar. This tradition involves devotion to, and the worship in various forms of, incarnated deities. The Hindu tradition is too vast and kaleidoscopic to be presented briefly. It involves the common store of an immense number of gods, both male and female, and their consorts and coteries, myths, practices, and festivals, that can be reframed, refashioned, and understood differently among the many Hindu subgroups and regions of India. Indeed, the approach to religious life itself and its place in the individual's life can differ greatly among different groups all identified as Hindu.

There is one significant unifying underlying commonality which, in truth, is beyond the purview of this book; but it is necessary for any broader understanding of Indian religiousness. This concept seems to have been present already in the thought world of the Vedas and continued through all the various iterations of the Hindu tradition. It seems to be presupposed in the teachings of both the Buddha and Mahavira as well. This is the constellation of ideas involving the system of castes (a hierarchy of social demarcations) into which one is born; *samsara* (reincarnation); the fulfillment of one's appropriate *dharma* (a complicated term to translate, but best understood as the interaction of the particular *dharma* of one's caste and life stage), which determines the accumulation of *karma* (popularly misunderstood as fate, but best translated as consequences—the consequences of one's discharge of their *dharma*), which determines whether one is reborn up or down in the caste system; and the ultimate goal of *moksha* (eventual liberation) from rebirth, which requires moving up to the top of the caste system and then off the wheel of rebirth.

One final expression of Indian religiousness—which will find itself alluded to in this book—is the Sikh tradition which was born in the fifteenth century as the result of the hostilities between the Hindu majority of the country and its Muslim rulers at the time. It is a syncretism—a blend—which incorporates elements of the Hindu constellation just mentioned with the monotheism of Islam. The Sikhs, too, play a prominent role in the religious tapestry of India today.

## The Goals of This Book

In this book we will be dealing with discrete elements of each of these traditions. Admittedly, the book will be an inadequate introduction to any of them; for that you may want to do more study on your own. What we will be doing here is, using phenomenology and other tools, exploring some ways in which parts of these traditions shed light on parts of the Jewish tradition. In some cases, information from India will give us a deeper understanding of aspects of our Torah. In others, it will shed light on aspects of Jewish practice which are part of Jewish life today. And in still others, we can recall ourselves to perhaps under-appreciated values that are part of our tradition. Together, by looking at our own familiar religious tradition in conversation with the very different traditions of India, we may come to see our tradition more clearly.

# chapter 1

# The gods and God

When we start to think about any possible encounter between the Jewish tradition and the Hindu tradition, the first glaring obstacle we encounter is the Jewish tradition's rigorous monotheism and the dazzling multiplicity of Hindu gods. What could possibly bridge so vast a chasm?

If you have ever had the chance to visit a Hindu temple, the first thing that strikes you is the many and varied images before which people are offering prayer. We will talk about the images themselves in the next chapter. What concerns us here is the very multiplicity. When we think of the Hindu tradition, we are likely to describe it as polytheistic. It is the manyness of the gods that strikes us. Actually, the reality is somewhat more complex than that. The truth is that there are many ways to be religiously Hindu.

It is possible to be a Hindu atheist.

To Christians, the notion of Hindu atheism may well strike the ear as discordant. That is because Christianity is a credal tradition. Christian identity is wholly dependent on belief. Whether you are a Christian at all depends on belief. Indeed, what you believe defines the type of Christian you are.

For Jews, the phrase may not sound dissonant at all; indeed, it may well have a familiar ring to it. The peculiar nature of Jewish identity—the fact that we are both a religious identity and a people—have made it a familiar reality to us to hear of Jewish atheists.

Some of the greatest Jews of our time have been atheists: people like David Ben Gurion, Albert Einstein, Sigmund Freud. All of them proud Jews, deeply committed to Jewish survival, immersed in Jewish culture, making significant contributions to Jewish life, and yet distant from what we would call religious faith.

Many Jewish families include both people of profound piety and very Jewishly-engaged atheists. So perhaps for us the idea of a Hindu atheist is not so confusing.

However it strikes our ears, the essential fact here is that it is possible to be a Hindu atheist. How could this possibly be the case? Haven't we already made reference to all those divinities represented in every Hindu temple? You may recall the constellation of beliefs involving reincarnation, *dharma*, *karma*, and *moksha/* liberation that were mentioned in the introduction. One way to look at this constellation is to see it as a steady state system: one that runs of its own accord with no need of outside control. The process can run without benefit of, indeed without any relation to, the gods. Of course, it is possible to connect the system to any one of the gods. But it is no less possible to conceive of it without any of them. Indeed, when the Buddha formulated his teaching, he made the atheism of his understanding of Indian religious tradition explicit. So, despite the multiplicity of deities we associate with the Hindu tradition, one way to be a Hindu is to be a Hindu and an atheist.

We have already made mention of the visual witness to how it is more than possible to be a Hindu polytheist. The number of gods who are invoked by Hindus is incalculable. From its very beginnings the religious tradition of India invoked numerous gods, in no systematic fashion. In the Vedas, we encounter Surya, the god of the sun; Agni, the god of fire; Indra, the god of thunderbolts, clouds, and rain; and Varuna, the god of the upper regions and of justice. These early gods, most of whom are no longer worshipped, seem to be personifications of elements of the natural world. They testify to the many aspects of the natural world which were threatening to earlier humans, or upon which these distant ancestors of ours depended. This multiplicity of gods, though not the identities of the many gods, has persisted through the millennia of Indian religious tradition.

Visitors to India today speak of being overwhelmed by the number of different deities whose statues, pictorial representations, and shrines confront them at every turn. Today, the *trimurti*, the triad of Brahma, Vishnu, and Shiva, are often referred to as the most significant of the gods, representing creation, preservation, and closure respectively. But they hardly exhaust the panoply of gods to whom people are devoted. And, indeed, people can worship any number of the many deities in any combination. As an example, one can hardly worship Shiva without also worshipping his wife Parvati and her son Ganesha, and/or his other wife Durga, or her alter ego, Kali, and any of the many deities associated with each of them. It seems that the list of deities to whom one can be devoted grows exponentially. Each of the gods has their consorts and cohort of associates. Different gods serve different functions. And people can turn to any of them for their specialized needs or simply because of their own idiosyncratic personalities. Given this, it is easy to see why Hindus are most conventionally described as polytheists.

But that does not exhaust the possibilities of Hindu religiousness. The fact is that it is also possible to be a Hindu monotheist. Indeed, in the recent past this became the subject of conversation between a group of prominent Hindu religious leaders and representatives of the Chief Rabbinate of the State of Israel. When the Chief Rabbinate was challenged about meeting with polytheists, something strictly forbidden by Jewish law, they responded that they were convinced by the Hindu leaders' assertion that they were monotheists. In a joint declaration, the participants in the meeting asserted:

> The participants reaffirmed their commitment to deepening the bilateral relationship predicated on the recognition of One Supreme Being, Creator and Guide of the Cosmos…. It is recognized that the One Supreme Being, both in its formless and manifest aspects has been worshipped by Hindus

for Millennia. This does not mean that Hindus worship "gods" and "idols." The Hindu relates to only the One Supreme Being when he/she prays to a particular manifestation.

—Declaration of the Second Hindu-Jewish
Leadership Summit 2008

This declaration may strike us as problematic. Is it possible that the representatives of the Chief Rabbinate were being disingenuous about being convinced? Or were they deceived? Could the Hindu spokesmen have misrepresented themselves? Certainly their representation of the Hindu tradition does not comport with what our eyes tell us about Hindu religiousness. As Chico Marx famously asked, "Who you gonna believe, me or your own eyes?" When it comes to Hindu monotheism, the reality is most complicated. Let us begin by acknowledging that the declaration reflects the understanding of one particular Hindu perspective. It hardly represents the understanding of all Hindus. Still, what is important is the reality that it is absolutely possible to be a Hindu monotheist. In fact, there are several ways.

A Hindu can simply believe that Brahma (or Shiva or Lakshmi or any of the gods) is the One Supreme Being. He or She alone is god. The others simply are not. This approach might certainly resonate for Jews. It has precedent in Jewish tradition. The subtext of the narrative of Moses in Egypt is that the God of the Hebrews is God, and the Pharaoh is not. Much later, the lesson of the prophet Elijah and his successors was that the Lord is God, not Baal. Perhaps Hindus who maintain this approach and Jews might find at least some measure of convergence in this.

Still another way of being a Hindu monotheist is the one articulated in the Upanishads, those commentaries on the Vedas which constitute the final layer of Vedic texts. It is not simply that there is only one God. Rather, the great truth is that God is everything. Everything that exists, ourselves included, is nothing but a manifestation of God. This understanding, which in India is called non-dualism, propounds the theology which is known in the West as Pantheism. This approach, too, has Jewish parallels. It is the philosophical core of the teaching of Benedict/Baruch Spinoza. More normatively, this is the idea at the heart of Lurianic Kabballah, the mystical stream of Jewish thought which finds its literary expression in the Zohar, and its communal expression in the various Chasidic movements. Jewish pantheists and Hindu pantheists might express their religious perspective in different words and different rituals. But at bottom they would recognize themselves in one another.

There is yet another way to be a Hindu monotheist, and it appears to be the perspective which the Hindu interlocutors with the Israeli Chief Rabbinate represent. Without dismissing the apparent multiplicity of gods, the monotheist of this approach asserts that there is only One Supreme Being, all the other gods that are worshipped are merely manifestations of that One Supreme Being. In other words, what may appear to be many gods are simply (somewhat inferior) representations of the single One. All the other gods are just expressions of Vishnu—or Durga, or Brahma, or any one of the myriad of gods. This perspective is most forcefully stated in the Bhagavad Gita, perhaps the most beloved of Hindu texts. In it the incarnated deity, Krishna, asserts:

> Those who are devotees of other gods,
> Worshipping them with sincere faith
> Are actually only worshipping me…
> Even if in an incorrect way.
> It is I who am the [real] recipient of all sacrifices
> Though…[those who worship other "gods"]
> Do not know me as I really am
> —Bhagavad Gita 9:23–24

It is this understanding of the apparent polytheism of Hindus transformed into a disguised monotheism that the interlocutors of the Israeli Chief Rabbinate represented as being the understanding of all Hindus. This is likely not the case. What we have seen, however, is that it is inarguable that, for many Hindus, in the various ways we have examined, what looks like polytheism is merely a scrim behind which can be found the reality of an underlying Hindu monotheism.

Thus far we have noted Hindu atheism, polytheism, and monotheism, finding in the first and last of these a certain resonance with some dimensions of Jewish thought. And yet these three options do not exhaust the possibilities of Hindu religiousness. It is in one last form of Hindu faith that we can find the richest opportunity to shed important light on one crucial aspect of Jewish religious tradition.

It is possible that the most prevalent form of Hindu religiousness is not the apparent polytheism that presents itself to our eyes or the monotheism of the intellectual elites. Rather, it is a perspective that falls somewhere between the two.

Most Hindus are most probably henotheists. And their henotheism offers us a rich opportunity for some deep Jewish reflection.

First, some words about henotheism itself. Like the polytheist, the henotheist recognizes the existence of many gods: the universe might be filled with gods. And, like the monotheist, the henotheist is committed to the fact that there is only one God *for me*. It is, of course, the *for me* that differentiates the henotheist from the polytheist, because it allows for the reality of other deities. It is only that those deities are irrelevant to the henotheist believer. I don't think it unfair to compare the henotheist to the faithful monogamist. It is not that there are not other women or men out there; but my spouse is the only one for me.

So, a Hindu may worship any one of the many potential objects of devotion with exclusivity. In this they do not deny the existence or reality of the gods that other people worship. But they do deny the relevance of those other beings *to them*. How does one settle on a particular god? They may be devotees of the god of their family, or their particular village, town, city or region. They might worship the god of their particular craft or profession. A particular god might be important to them at one particular stage of their life (students tend to revere the elephant-headed god Ganesha—after all, elephants never forget), or when they are dealing with a particular set of issues (women with fertility issues will pray to Lakshmi for children). While they are devotees of that god, the other gods, while real, are of no importance to them.

Things change. People move from a village to the town, or from one city to another. They might change professions, grow up, or resolve the issue that drew them to a particular god. At such a time, they might shift their allegiances, become devotees of another god. At that point the henotheist, unlike the polytheist, will not simply go on worshipping the first god and add a second to the roster. They would have to take leave of the former object of their devotion and establish an exclusive relationship with the god who is now more appropriate for their life situation. Most Hindus appear to be functionally, if not ideologically, henotheists. They live in special relationship to one, and only one, god at a time. The people whom we call Hindu are likely not to use that term to define themselves. It was imposed upon them by conquerors from other cultures. They are more likely to identify themselves as devotees of Shiva (or Krishna, or Hanuman, or any of the many gods they could be worshipping), without denying the existence of any, or all, of those other gods. That is the essence of henotheism. And it is to an encounter with this henotheism and its potential significance in an understanding of Jewish religiousness that we now turn.

How could any of this have any relevance to Jewish religion, given that Jews have always been rigorously monotheistic? This encounter with the henotheistic dimension of the Hindu tradition opens the door for us to examine our assumptions about our own religious tradition. I suggest we examine biblical theology the same way that archaeologists examine biblical history. If you have visited Israel, you are familiar with the geographical feature called the *tel*. To the untrained eye it looks like nothing so much as another small hill. But an archaeologist would recognize it immediately as an artificial mound created by the piling up, century after century, of the ruins of city upon city over millennia. When you climb to the top of the *tel*, you might find a soda can, last week's newspaper, a discarded automobile tire. Those are extremely recent and not at all relevant to the story that the *tel* can reveal. If, like a trained archaeologist, you make a cut, dig a shaft, you will uncover the secrets the *tel* is holding. The material you will excavate closer to the top of the cut are remains of a more recent city and civilization. The further down you go, the more ancient the city and civilization you are dealing with. The more revelatory material is further down.

We can explore our Torah like a *tel*. Much as we like to think of our sacred text as monolithic, all of a piece, the more exciting reality is that the Torah contains material that reflects different periods and perspectives, artfully joined together through an editorial process. If we examine our Torah this way, we can actually see the evolution of biblical theology. The monotheism we take for granted as *always rigorously* being the theology of our people, is actually closer to the top of our Torah *tel*. I doubt that even at the very bottom of the shaft we would find an official ideology of polytheism (not that many of the people did not embrace those practices—see, for one example among many II Kings 23:10. Why do you think the prophets kept on excoriating them for it?—see, for instance, Ezekiel 8:16–17). But having appreciated the role of henotheism in the Hindu tradition, I believe that at the earliest layers of the Torah, the earliest layers of the theology of the Jewish people, we will find there too, the presence of henotheism.

Once our encounter with henotheism in India has accustomed our eyes to henotheism, we find it hiding in plain sight when we read the Torah. Henotheism offers us an Ockham's razor (the simplest explanation is most likely the correct one) with which to read verses and phrases that confound our understanding or which we struggle to interpret allegorically. When read in the light of what we have seen in India, these verses reveal to us that at some early point in biblical history, our ancestors' theological perspective was henotheism. They did not worship other gods, but they did not deny that those other gods existed. They acknowledged them, while maintaining an exclusive relationship with the Lord, their God, who was the One God...for them.

Several salient examples of familiar verses that take on significantly different meaning when viewed in this light.

> Who is like You among the gods, O Lord,
> Who is like You exalted in holiness.

If the words seem somewhat familiar it is because they have been incorporated into the liturgy of our worship services. The words are given here in their literal meaning, though when they appear in our Prayer Books translators struggle to make them fit with today's theological understanding. They are from Exodus 15:11, a poem of victory called the Song of the Sea, which is conventionally regarded as among the oldest sections of the Torah. The simplest understanding of this famous verse is that among all the existing gods, none is greater, more exalted than the Lord, the God of the Hebrews. The acceptance of the reality of other gods is clear, as is the affirmation of a special relationship between the people and this particular deity.

In Genesis 31:53, we read about a pact made between the patriarch Jacob, and his uncle and father-in-law Laban. They take an oath of mutual respect. Its formula deserves our attention:

> May the God of Abraham and the God of Nahor
> keep justice between us....and Jacob swore by ...
> the God of his father Isaac.

In this oath and this pact, we see a tacit recognition of the god of another people, juxtaposed, once again, to Israel's exclusive relationship to its own God.

The religious perspective here clearly cannot be called monotheistic, but properly must be seen as henotheistic.

Even if our knowledge of the Torah is limited, we all are acquainted with the Ten Commandments. But perhaps we have not reflected on the complexity of the familiar words of the first injunction of those Commandments:

> I the Lord am your God...
> You shall have no other gods beside me.

What should strike us in these words is what is asserted and what is not asserted. This famous formulation does not deny the reality of those other gods. It does not say what we might expect it to assert: "there are no other gods" or "other gods do not exist." Rather it seems to tacitly recognize that there are other gods. What it does demand is that our ancestors not worship those gods. Again, it stresses not the impossibility of other gods, but the exclusivity of the people's relationship with its God—the singularity of the Lord's claim on Israel.

Everything that we have just said about this first injunction in the Ten Commandments applies to an injunction later in the Book of Exodus, that is even more graphic, 34:14–15:

> You shall not bow down to another god. For the
> Lord's name is jealous. He is a jealous God. Lest

you make a covenant with the inhabitants of the
land and go whoring after their gods.

Once again, the image we are left with is that different people are
understood to have different gods. Those gods are not depicted as
non-existent. Faith in them is not asserted to be misguided; merely
inappropriate for the people of Israel.

One more example, perhaps the most disruptive of our conventional assumptions. It comes from Psalm 82. Translators have
struggled to render it idiomatically so that it corresponds to our
current theological posture. But translated literally 82:1 and 6–7
say:

> God is located in the assembly of gods
> In the midst of the gods He judges....
> "I had said, 'You were gods,
> Sons of the Most High, all of you
> But you shall die like humans
> Like one of the[ir] princes shall you fall.'"

Quite a remarkable image. Here, God is depicted as presiding
over a gathering of, dare we say it, other divine beings, albeit He
is depicted as occupying a superior position. As the rest of the
psalm makes clear, He is chastising them for their failure to promote justice. And as a consequence, He is demoting them. No
longer can they continue to be deities. The difficulty traditional
translators and commentators face is how markedly this vignette
clashes with our current theology. Clearly, though, it reflects an
outlook in which the Lord, the God of Israel, coexists with other
divine beings. Perhaps this narrative episode reflects the end of
that phase of Israelite theology, when the "other gods" were losing
their significance and making way for the time when there would

be not merely "one God for you," but One God. Nonetheless, the striking image of this psalm clearly hearkens back to a time further down our Torah *tel*, a time when the people were not yet monotheistic.

What have we learned? I hope the evidence has convinced you that, at some early point in their life as a people, the people of Israel were, like many Hindus today, henotheists. Should this disturb you, or cause you to dismiss the Torah? I cannot understand why it would. If anything, it should give us all greater reason to be awed by the Torah. Read in this way, it is a profound and moving record of how the people of Israel grew in their understanding. Rather than simply being handed the *fait accompli* of the monotheistic idea, it was the collective genius of the people to evolve to a deeper understanding of the nature of the God they worshipped. The Torah, read in this light, is shown to be a record of the unfolding of the most important idea in Jewish religiousness.

The full unfolding of that idea seems to have taken place during the period of the prophets. Perhaps that is their greatest contribution to the tradition that drew from them. We will return to that shortly. But before we do, we can look at the full flowering of the monotheistic idea which we find a good bit higher up in our Torah *tel*—in the seventh century BCE. The words of the prophet Isaiah 44:6; 45:21–22 and Deuteronomy 32:39 were written around the same time:

> Thus says the Lord, the King of Israel
> And his redeemer....
> I am the first and I am the last,
> And beside Me, there is not god
>
> (Isaiah 44:6)

There is no other god beside me....
For I am God and there is none else

(Isaiah 45:21–22)

See, then, that I, I am He
There is no god beside Me.
I deal death and I give life
I wound and I heal
There is none to deliver from my hand

(Deuteronomy 32:39)

Here we find a clear, and stirring, expression of the ultimate triumph of monotheism in Israel. Indeed, we can almost feel like we are present at the historical moment when the henotheism that had characterized the people's theology at an earlier time was displaced and the monotheistic faith, which we think of as "always," now becomes the core principle of Jewish religiousness.

This displacement of henotheism by monotheism is, of course, important in the unfolding of Jewish theology. It also played a crucial role in the history of the Jewish people. It answers a number of riddles:

What happened to the "ten lost tribes" of Israel?

Why did the citizens of kingdom of Judah continue to exist as a people when the citizens of the kingdom of Israel did not?

Why are there still Jews in the world?

To begin to answer these questions, we must take a step back. We have been looking at the period when the official theology of Israel was not yet monotheistic. Israelites were henotheists. But we have not yet taken note of the fact that, as best as archaeologists can determine, they were not alone in their henotheism. The entire region they lived in was henotheistic too. And what the henotheists of the ancient Near East believed is crucial to understanding this last period of biblical history.

The Israelites and their neighbors believed that every nation had its own territory and its own god. When you entered the territory of any people, you also entered the territory of that people's god. Whomever you may have worshipped in your homeland is now irrelevant. You owe your allegiance to the deity in whose territory you now found yourself. As we have noted in India, gods can be changed when circumstances change. It was also believed that, when nations went to war with one another, as, apparently, they constantly did, the gods of those respective nations also went to war. You knew which god had won by learning which nation won. The winning god was clearly the more powerful (perhaps you hear echoes of Exodus 15:11 in this). If you were in the unfortunate position of being on the losing side, you were, if you were not killed, likely taken into slavery in the victors' land. At that point, you would no longer be devoted to the god of your homeland—who, in any event, was revealed to be less powerful than the god of the victors in whose land you were now enslaved. And you would transfer your allegiance to the god of that land. Those were what we can call the rules of the game in the ancient Near East. The Israelites, just like their neighbors, knew them and played by them.

In this worldview, the land that the kingdom of Israel and the kingdom of Judah—the existence of two kingdoms being the result of a political division after the death of King Solomon—occupied was their assigned territory. And the God that they worshipped was the God of that land. But catastrophe struck in the year 722 BCE. The king of Israel, having made a serious political miscalculation, was attacked by the nation of Assyria, and defeated. His subjects were taken captive to Assyria and … disappeared. What happened to them? Over the years travelers have searched for—and some claim to have found—the "ten lost tribes." They are the Lakota Sioux of America, or the Pashtun of Afghanistan or the Lembaa of Zimbabwe, and many more. The reality is less dramatic than that. Having been conquered and taken to Assyria, the rules of the game demanded that they become proper Assyrians and worship the god of Assyria. Apparently, some, perhaps already moving in the direction of monotheism, or perhaps simply more invested in their Israelite identity, abandoned the rules and somehow made their way back to their homeland and became subjects of the king of Judah: archaeologists say that the population of the city of Jerusalem doubled around this time. The rest are not "lost" at all. They simply continued to play by the rules and disappeared into Assyrian society.

It was after the destruction of the kingdom of Israel, in the remaining kingdom of Judah, perhaps precipitated by the catastrophe, that monotheism began to displace the henotheistic theology. The religion of the remaining Israelites had become a monotheistic one. And so it was that when the last king of Judah, having made his own political miscalculation, was attacked and defeated by Babylonia in 586 BCE, the old rules no longer applied. People now understood that their defeat was not the result of the god of the Babylonians defeating their God. Rather, it was the result of the will of the One God—now the only God—who used the armies of Babylonia to punish them for their own unfaithfulness. By the time they arrived in Babylonia, a new religious perspective dominated. There was no defeated god and no victorious god. They had no need to forsake their God and embrace the god of Babylonia. Monotheism had triumphed and they, unlike the earlier citizens of the kingdom of Israel, did not disappear into the host culture. They maintained their identity and their faith in the One God and found ways to worship that God on alien soil. Testimony to that transformation is found in Psalm 137 which asks a rhetorical henotheistic question and responds with a monotheistic answer:

> By the rivers of Babylon there we sat and wept
>   when we remembered Zion.

There on the poplars
  we hung our harps,
for there our captors asked us for songs,
  our tormentors demanded songs of joy;
  they said, "Sing us one of the songs of Zion!"
How can we sing the songs of the Lord
  while in a foreign land?
If I forgot you, Jerusalem,
  may my right hand forget its skill.
May my tongue cling to the roof of my mouth
  if I remember you not,
if I do not consider Jerusalem
  above my highest joy.

"How could I sing of the God of Israel here in Babylonia?" is a natural question under the henotheistic rules of the game. The retort, "If I forgot Jerusalem," is the answer of a monotheist whose faith and identity are no longer conducted in terms of that earlier understanding. The former inhabitants of Judah had moved on.

The newly monotheistic exiles in Babylon, released from the henotheistic restriction of their religious life to their homeland, were now freed to adapt their ancient traditions to a diaspora setting. The evolution from henotheism to monotheism released them to innovate and adapt their ancestral lore and practices in ways that would allow the religion of Judah to be transformed into Judaism: a Judaism that would endure long beyond the biblical period.

One concluding thought. The henotheism that characterized the earliest stages of biblical thought also helps us deal with one of Jewish tradition's thorniest issues: the problem of how to understand the idea of chosenness. It has been framed politely, "How odd of God to choose the Jews," and not at all politely in the vituperative claims over the millennia that Jews somehow regard themselves as superior to other people and are thus worthy objects of resentment and hatred. Jews, themselves, have struggled with the presumptuousness that the idea of being chosen can imply. One great Jewish thinker, Mordecai Kaplan, wrote a prayerbook from which all references to chosenness have been expunged (though it should be noted that for this and other reasons, Kaplan's Prayer Book was burned and Kaplan, himself, excommunicated by the Orthodox authorities of the time). Much ink has been spilled trying to ameliorate the assumed offensiveness of the idea or explain it in ways that dilutes its presumed toxicity.

The henotheism of the early stages of the Bible gives us a different perspective from which to address this issue. The so-called choosing of the Israelite people was hardly an audacious innovation. It was, rather, merely an artifact of the general ideology of henotheism in the ancient near east. In that cultural universe, all peoples were seen as privileged inhabitants of their allotted territory, and all were considered to be the recipients of their god's special attention and concern. In other words, in the intellectual world out of which the Torah emerged, every people was seen as chosen by its god, just as every population was "chosen" by its king. Rather than being a unique and uniquely self-aggrandizing proposition of the Israelite people, it was simply their rendition of the shared world-view of that time and place. Theirs, however, was the only one to be incorporated in a literature that survived into later times.

We have travelled quite a distance. From exploring particular ways in which one can be Hindu, we found ourselves engaged in an unexpected exploration of biblical theology, and the consequences of the Babylonian exile of the citizens of Judah. We have unlocked the story of the evolution of the biblical understanding of God, using the henotheistic stream of Hindu religiousness as a key. This highlights the emergence of monotheism as the dominant ideology of the Torah, which enabled Judaism to survive as the religious expression of a people living outside their ancestral homeland.

# chapter 2

# Depicting God:
# Graven Images and Mythology

Hindu and Jewish traditions have many diverse elements. In the last chapter, we talked about the fact that, in the Hindu tradition, any god is likely to be one among many; while in the Jewish tradition, while that might have been the case farther down our *tel* of the Torah, by the end of the biblical period, God was understood as One. But the gap between the two traditions is not measured only in numbers. In this chapter, we will discuss another set of issues that divides them: mythology and iconography—how the divine is described and depicted, what stories are told about the divine, and how the deity is visually represented. Dwelling on these issues can help Jews appreciate what is unique about the Jewish monotheism that we might take for granted.

## Graven Images

"Jewish civilization has not fostered the creation of art, because the second commandment forbids it." It is a rare achievement for one sentence to be false for three different reasons. Perhaps we should award some kind of prize to this one, repeated frequently by people who ought to know better. In the first place, Jews have produced great art (do the names Chagall, Soutine or Modigliani ring any bells?), indeed great religious art (the mosaics from the first century Bet Alpha synagogue in Israel, the frescoes of the Dura-Europos synagogue in Syria, the Sarajevo Haggadah, and a host of others). The second commandment does not prohibit graphic representations. At most it can be read as a prohibition of three-dimensional art. And—finally—it is, in fact, not even a prohibition of sculptural art, except for such images created to be worshipped—"do not bow down to them or worship them" (Exodus 20:5). Worshipping and creating are two very different things. Jewish religious scholars resolved this issue long ago. Already in the twelfth century one sage, Jacob ben Reuben, wrote:

> Our Creator, may He be praised, never forbade the production of statues or pictures. He only forbade them with respect to worship and service. ... But Scripture never forbade the making of images or the act of beautifying some work or building.
> (Sefer Milchamot ha-Shem, 57)

The fact of the matter is, the misreading of the Jewish relationship to art assumes that Jewish tradition is radically aniconic: opposed to any representational imagery. In this we might say that the purveyors of this error are confusing Jews with Muslims. A visitor to almost any synagogue would find all manner of artistic creations: photographs, oil painting, perhaps stained-glass windows of biblical (or other) scenes, and, yes, even sculpture. The same cannot be said of mosques. Muslims, unlike Jews, are scrupulous in not decorating their houses of worship with representational depictions of anything from the world of nature. That does not prevent them from being beautiful spaces. Many of the great architectural jewels of the world are mosques. Rich materials, ornate carving, magnificent carpets, the splendid use of light, make them spiritually uplifting, even for the non-Muslim. What they do not have are representational depictions of human scenes, or elements of the natural world. In place of these, you are more likely to find splendid calligraphic quotations from the Qur'an and abstract images drawn from the vegetative world.

What Jews and Muslims do share is a hard and fast avoidance of depicting the God they worship. Whatever art you will find in a synagogue—even in pictures of biblical scenes—, you are unlikely to find any depiction of God. Moses carrying the ten commandments, of course. God handing Moses the Ten Commandments, absolutely not. And certainly, any Muslim house of worship or religious text would be even more rigorous in this norm. Not only would God, or the angel Gabriel, not be depicted in transmitting revelation to the Prophet Muhammad; Muhammad would not be depicted in receiving it.

In this regard, Jews and Muslims are radically different from some streams of the other Abrahamic tradition. While there are some Christian denominations that are as radically opposed to iconography as Muslims, in the "high" traditions Orthodox and many other Christian houses of worship are renowned for the magnificence of the art contained in them. Stained glass windows, paintings, statues: all are familiar elements of the great cathedrals and the humble parish church. In these Christian houses of worship, there is no restraint in depicting elements of the natural world, or human beings. But what separates them from both the more art-embracing Jewish synagogues and the aniconic Muslim mosques is the absence of any inhibition in depicting the divine. The depictions of Jesus—the third person of the trinity according to most Christian teaching—is ubiquitous. But an even greater gap between Christians and their fellow members of the family of Abraham is the Christian willingness to depict the deity whom Christians would call God the Father. Christian art of various kinds depicts God in biblical scenes (think the Sistine chapel) and a host of other contexts. Pictures of the deity are displayed in Christian homes with no compunction, something that would be unthinkable for Jews or Muslims.

With that single, not incidental, exception, the Jewish tradition is one that has been open to, and embracing of, the visual arts. Nonetheless, even with that openness, we can expect that when it comes to sacred images, the gap between the Jewish and Hindu traditions would be vast. Indeed, we can imagine that because of this gap, committed Jews might find it difficult to engage with the Hindu tradition, and might insist that such engagement is impossible. Why would this be the case? Perhaps the greatest reason for this potential disengagement is the centrality of images in Hindu worship.

In our last chapter, we made a virtual visit to a Hindu temple. It was pungent with the scent of burning incense, elaborately decorated, and had at its focal point an array of brightly colored and richly adorned images of the special deities of the particular subset of Hindus whose temple this was. Most often, we would find the image of one principal god and somewhat smaller images of the retinue of gods associated with him or her. There is no denying it, the images are glorious. Beautifully designed, extravagantly colorful, they are aesthetically compelling and a visual testimony to the devotion of the people who worship before them and make offerings to them.

If you have visited even the greatest and most storied Christian cathedral, you will find, upon leaving, in the back of the sanctuary, a gift shop where the faithful can purchase candles, rosaries, crucifixes, or other religious objects, to serve both to enrich the visitor's faith life and as a souvenir of the visit. It is as likely to be true of humbler churches, and no small number of synagogues as well. Our virtual visit to a Hindu temple is about to conclude. On our way out, we will pass through ... a gift shop, where we—as well as the Hindu pilgrim—will be offered the opportunity to purchase a smaller version of the images we saw in the prayer hall—and other images as well—for our own personal use.

This reminds us just how essential the images are to Hindu religious life. Their use is not limited exclusively to temples. In India and other Hindu countries, images of the gods are omnipresent in shrines that dot roadsides and city streets. More significantly, every Hindu home has its own family shrine, usually in the northeast corner of the house, at which puja—worship and offering—is done every day, most usually by the matriarch of the family, on behalf of her entire household. The family shrine is every bit as much a sacred space as the more public temple complexes. Indeed, it is used much more frequently and with no less fervor. At sacred times—on festivals and special occasions—, the family will gather at the shrine or move the image from the shrine to another specially prepared space in the house to make offerings and recite prayers together. In each of these cases, puja is impossible to conceive without the presence of the revered image. The image is not an incidental component of religious life for most Hindus. Indeed, it is not an overstatement to identify the image as central.

The Jewish response to the role of images in Hindu religiousness is unequivocal. It has a long history. The second commandment which we referred to earlier may not prohibit the creation of art. But it is unequivocal in forbidding the fashioning of images to be worshipped. (Exodus 20:4–5). That prohibition is repeated later in the same book, "You shall not make molten gods for yourselves" (Exodus 34:17). That injunction is reinforced in the narrative of the golden calf, which the Israelites had fashioned for themselves by Moses' brother, Aaron, and which they worshipped with the incantation, "this is your God, O Israel who brought you up out of the land of Egypt," and for which they were excoriated and punished (Exodus 32). The Book of Leviticus is filled with specific injunctions on the subject:

> Do not turn to idols or make molten gods for
> yourselves. I am the Lord your God.
>
> (Leviticus 19:4)

> You shall not make idols for yourselves or set up
> for yourselves carved images or pillars, or place
> figured stones in your land to worship them, for I
> the Lord am your God.
>
> (Leviticus 26:1)

Later in the history of the people, the prophet Isaiah crafted some mordant satires of the practice of making—and worshipping—idols:

> I am the Lord, that is my name
> And My glory I will not give to another,
> Neither My praise to graven images.
>
> (Isaiah 42:8)

> Who has fashioned a god or molten image
> That is profitable for nothing?...
> He plants a bay-tree, and the rain nourishes it.
> Then a man uses it for fuel,
> And he takes some of it and warms himself;
> He uses it for a fire and bakes breads
> [and with the remainder]
> He makes a god and worships it;
> He makes a graven image and falls down to it.
> He burns half of it in the fire
> And roasts some meat and is satisfied;
> He warms himself with it and says "ah,"
> I am warm, I have seen the fire
> With the rest of it he makes a god,
> even his graven image
> he falls down to it, and worships it,
> and prays to it
> and says "deliver me, for you are my god"
> They know nothing. They do not understand.
>
> (Isaiah 44:10, 14–18)

We cannot help but wonder who is it that Isaiah says knows nothing and understands nothing. Is it the idols which have been manufactured? Or the people who worship them? Isaiah continues his satirical denunciation of idols:

[God says], "to whom will you compare Me
Declare me similar?
You only squander gold from your purse
Or weigh out silver on the balance
When you hire a metal worker to turn it into a god
To which you bow down and worship.
You have to carry it on your backs to transport it.
Piled as a burden on tired beasts and cattle…
When you put it down it just stands there.
It does not budge from its place.
When you cry out, it does not answer.
It cannot save you from your distress.

(Isaiah 46:1, 5–7)

Even the sublime Book of Psalms writes of idols, and their makers, in the same derisive tone:

Their idols are silver and gold,
    the work of men's hands.
They have mouths, but they speak not;
    eyes have they, but they see not.
They have ears, but they hear not;
    noses have they, but they smell not.
They have hands, but they grasp not;
    feet have they, but they walk not.
Nor do they speak with their throat.
Those who made them shall be just like them,
    Every one that trusts them.
O Israel, trust in the Lord,
    He [is the One who] is your help and your shield.

(Psalm 115:4–9)

These biblical texts, and others like them, established the paradigm for later Jewish understandings of what the Jewish tradition invariably refers to as idols.

The rabbis, who wrote after the Torah was completed, lived in the context of Roman civilization and religion. They were unsparing in their condemnation of idolatry and identified it as one of the three most heinous transgressions, along with sexual immorality and murder. Though they were in no position to impose legal penalties, they deemed these three crimes to be capital offenses.

The most graphic of the rabbis' denunciation of idolatry is found in a series of midrashim—rabbinic elaborations of a Torah narrative. The rabbis ponder Abraham's actions in Genesis 12, when God calls on Abraham to leave everything he has known ("your homeland, your father's house, and the place of your birth"—in other words, his entire past) and go to the unknown "land that I will show you." They ask, as we would, why did Abraham agree with such alacrity? They wonder how Abraham could have had such trust in God. They note the fact that in the text we never actually see the point at which Abraham "met" God, came to know God and trust God so completely that he would immediately agree to God's command.

The rabbis' answer was to fashion several narratives about the life of Abraham in the period before Genesis 12. In one of the narratives, Abraham reasons his way from worshipping the multiple forces of nature to the One who is behind all those phenomena. In the stories that are of interest to us here, Abraham's father, Terach, is a maker of idols. One day he leaves Abraham in charge of his idol workshop and gallery. As various customers come to purchase his wares, Abraham denounces them in very personal terms for their gullibility—"Don't you know that these pieces of wood and stone can do nothing? I watched my father manufacture them!"

In another midrash that is so well-known even among Jews to this day that many assume it is included in the Book of Genesis itself—which it is not—Abraham's father again leaves Abraham in charge of his wares. While Terach is gone, Abraham takes a stick and smashes all the idols, leaving only the largest of them intact, and places the offending stick in the hand of the surviving idol. When Terach returns, he is appalled and demands to know what happened to reduce his merchandise to rubble. Abraham (unlike George Washington, who, when confronted with the unfortunate cherry tree situation, "could not tell a lie" to his father) tells his father that the largest of the idols flew into a rage and smashed the others to bits. Terach (with the same understanding of his handiwork as the rabbis and perhaps conveying their sense that an idol maker must be possessed of a certain degree of cynicism) tells Abraham that his excuse is nonsense: "that big idol cannot have smashed up the others. He cannot do anything at all. I made him myself." To which Abraham has the last word: "If he cannot even move enough to smash other idols with a stick, how can you worship it as the creator of heaven and earth?"

These two midrashim about Abraham in his father's shop, along with the satirical depictions of Isaiah and the Psalms, embody the Jewish tradition's attitude to what it dismisses as "idols" and "idol worship." And they undoubtedly reflect the way Jewish tradition perceives the prevalent image worship of Hindus. Unfortunately, this perception, with its millennia-old pedigree in Jewish thought, presents us with a dilemma. This traditional depiction suffers from one serious defect: it does not reflect, or do justice to, the actions or understanding of people who actually employ images in their worship life.

Let us resume our virtual visit to a Hindu temple. On our way out, as we pass through the gift shop, we notice a stylishly groomed woman with a tilaka (a sandalwood paste mark on her forehead indicating her sectarian affiliation), carefully examining several of the images on the shelves. We watch as she weighs the merits of a few different images of the god Krishna. After much deliberation, she selects one of them over the others. She has it wrapped up securely and carries it to her home to be installed in her personal shrine. Are we to imagine that this woman actually believes that the image she gently carried home from the temple gift shop was really responsible for creating "the heavens, and the earth, the sea and all that is in them?"

If our virtual trip to India has been planned properly, we will find ourselves in Mumbai (the city formerly known as Bombay) during the Hindu month of Bhadra (late summer/early fall). This way we will be able to participate in the festival of Ganesh Chaturthi, which is a ten-day celebration of the god Ganesha. You may remember him as the elephant-headed son of Shiva and Parvati. Preparations for this celebration begin with a visit to one of the many shops selling special unfired clay images of the god. Family groups lovingly escort the image back to their homes, where they have arranged and decorated a special shrine where the honored guest will stay for the ten days. During the festival, the family will gather, perhaps with the help of a Brahmin priest, to chant prayers and make offerings of gifts to the god.

Public worship will take place in the temples of the city, and public events of various kinds will be offered as well. Huge images of Ganesha will be paraded through the city. At the end of the festival, families will carry their image of the god to the shore. Large processions will accompany the huge public images as well. The festival ends as all these images of Ganesha are ceremoniously carried into the water. As people bid the god farewell, the images, being made of unfired clay, dissolve. The god has visited the city and their respective homes for ten days, and now has left them as they look forward to his return next year.

But let us step back a bit from what we have seen. How are we to really understand what we have witnessed in Mumbai? Could all of these images—in all these many homes; the huge ones and small ones—all actually be the reality of the god to whom their prayers were directed? Do gods dissolve when borne into the sea? Hindus can explain that the image is precisely that—an image. It is a testimony to the god to whom they are devoted. Something of the god may temporarily enter its image in their home. But that god is not co-existent with it. The image certainly helps the worshipper focus their attention on the god who is, in actuality, beyond it. But the devotee understands that in the end, while the god persists, the image before which they have been praying dissolves. The god endures, its image is no more.

This is a far cry from the way our Jewish forebears have led us to believe image worship worked. And it leaves us wondering: did the "idol worshippers" of the biblical period or of Rome believe what Isaiah and the rabbis ascribed to them? Or did they understand their practice in the same way as the Hindus of Mumbai? What were Isaiah, the Psalmist, and the rabbis up to? Is it possible that they simply did not understand the phenomenon of image worship? Or were they simply engaged in hyperbole as they satirized the worship practices of their neighbors?

I would suggest that they all knew very well what they were doing. What the prophets and the rabbis were engaged in was polemics. They were making a forceful distinction between their religious perspective and another. But the point that they were making was not simply about idol worship. That was merely one expression of the opposing ideology. What they were really concerned about involved not only iconography, but also narrative. Both the prophets and the rabbis were reacting to cultures that made use of images of their gods, and also told rich and complex stories about those gods, just as Hindus do. And their polemic was directed against a religious understanding that expressed itself not only through the visual representations of the gods but also through the tapestry of graphic narratives about them.

## Mythology

A word about terminology. In our everyday speech, the word *mythology* means something that is not true. This very morning, I saw a newspaper article headlined, "Five Food Myths," which identified things that people believe about diet which are false—including, to my personal relief, "Myth # 1: Sugar is addictive." That is not what it means in the study of religion. And that is not what it will mean here. As students of religion use the term, mythology means a narrative which is not told to convey scientific or historical realities, but which is intended to convey some underlying truth that is of profound importance to the teller and the hearer. All, some, or none, of the narrative elements of the narrative may not be what we call empirically true. And yet the myth is intended to convey a life-shaping truth.

The Hindu tradition offers a wealth of information and stories about its many gods. We are privy to the relationships and interactions of the gods, their alliances and friendships, and their hostilities and angers. Each of the gods has a library of elaborate stories told about them. We learn about births, life-struggles, disappointments, and achievements. We learn of their likes and dislikes, and how they prefer to spend their time. We see them engaged in courtship and battle. Each of them is the subject of a vast body of stories.

Each of the gods is described in precise detail. We are given clearcut descriptions of their appearance, their clothing, their weapons of choice, and perhaps the place of their residence. And, perhaps most significantly, stories are told of the various gods incarnating themselves in human, and other, forms. The gods of the Hindus seem to revel in taking shape and revealing themselves corporeally. The literary skill of generations is lavished on creating a clearly defined image of the deities. All of which is to say, we see the gods of the Hindus represented narratively in words just as they are rendered visually in the images. Let us make do with a few examples which will have to stand in for the many more which could fill hundreds of volumes.

One day Shiva's wife Parvati came back from her exertions. Before she bathed, she fashioned a boy from the dirt on her body and assigned him the task of guarding her privacy. While she was bathing, her husband, the fierce god Shiva, returned and demanded entrance. Neither the boy nor Shiva knew who the other one was. The boy, discharging his duty, refused to let Shiva enter. Shiva, in a rage, not knowing that this was Parvati's son, took out his sword and cut off the boy's head. When Parvati became aware of what happened to her son, she insisted that Shiva restore him to life. Shiva sent his minions to bring back the first head that they could find to place on the boy. They soon came back with the head of an elephant. With that, Shiva restored the now elephant-headed boy to life. Which is why Parvati's and Shiva's son, Ganesha, has the body of a boy and the head of an elephant.

We could spend much time exploring the non-theological meaning of this story. The narrative vibrates with psychological undertones, including erotic tension. We also see expressions of maternal concern, and male volatility and aggressiveness. It addresses the inner dynamics of family life and also explores the consequences of a certain capriciousness while being endowed with power. The more we look at it, the more human it becomes.

Let us look at one more story. When the god Vishnu was incarnated as a human baby named Krishna, he was placed in the care of a human couple named Nanda and Yashoda. The parents had no idea that their baby was an incarnated deity and treated him just like a normal human baby. One day baby Krishna was crawling around on the ground and did what any normal baby would do. He found a clump of dirt and popped it into his mouth, And Nanda and Yashoda did what any normal parents would do, they ran after the baby, picked him up, and pried open his mouth to pull the dirt out. But when they opened up Krishna's mouth, something extraordinary occurred. They were overwhelmed by the sight of the entire cosmos, all of creation, everything that existed on the earth, in the heavens, in the seas, even in the realms of the gods. At which point they understood that they had been entrusted with no ordinary baby.

The story is a charming one, and despite its deep theological message, so relatable: a baby and its parents, the most domestic of settings. What baby does not behave in mischievous and un-predictable ways—also ways that are likely to provoke fear, even terror, in its parents? But also, and here is the most human part of the story, what parent does not look at their baby and see it as the sum and substance of all creation ("you are everything to me")?

What we have seen in these stories is, in narrative form, the same sort of graphic representation of the gods we experience in visual form in the images before which people do puja. The prophets and the rabbis do not rail against such stories in the same way they mock the images. But if we reflect on Jewish sa-cred texts, it becomes clear that Jewish tradition has (largely) dispensed with them as well. Encountering narratives such as these in texts sacred to Hindus might give us the opportunity to reflect on something about our own sacred texts that we had not seen as clearly before.

If we look at the Torah (and it will be the Torah that is the focus of our attention here) in the light of the Hindu sacred texts, some-thing will stand out in sharpened relief. The rabbis, as we shall note again later, did add layers of mythology to the Torah narrative. Normative Judaism in later generations tended to return to a less mythological mode in talking about God. In the context of these sacred texts of the Hindus, we are struck by a glaring absence. For a sacred scripture, the Torah has remarkably little to say about God. Beyond notably few portions where God is presented in human-like terms, God is hardly described. God is certainly not discussed systematically. We get little sense of God's internal life.

And, most significantly, God, on God's own, has no adventures, no exploits, no life independent of God's engagement with us.

We only see God when God is interacting with people. We are given no "backstory," no inkling of God's origins, no discussion of what God does when God is not attending to the people of Israel. In this regard, the Torah is strikingly different from the sacred texts of the Hindus. It is what we might call unmythological: it is not narratively rich when it comes to the life of the deity. There are simply no good stories about God in the Torah on par with the stories of the Hindus (or of Israel's various neighboring civilizations in Mesopotamia or Egypt—or of Rome in the time of the rabbis). The absence of narratives about God, especially in the Torah (admittedly, at a later time, the rabbis did add richer narrative dimensions to their teaching than the Torah itself included), resonate with the absence of Jewish figurative representations of the divine.

The Jewish satirical misrepresentation of image worship is of a piece with the relative scarcity of narratives about the divine in much of Jewish sacred literature. We can learn about Jewish religious thought by viewing it in the light of the visually and narratively rich traditions of the Hindus. Without seeing it in the context of this very different tradition, we might perhaps not notice the outlines of, or fully appreciate, what is unique in the character of Jewish religiousness.

The Jewish religious ideology that is highlighted for us when we see it in such contrast, is one that does not merely forcefully reject images of the divine or dispense with extensive mythological narrative about God. We learn, more consequentially, that Jewish monotheism is not merely a matter of numbers. Its core principle is not simply that God is numerically one. Rather, for Jewish monotheism, the assertion that God is one means that God is singular, unique, unlike God's creation in every way. In rejecting images and mythologies, Jewish monotheism is insistent on God's incorporeality. God is radically dissimilar to anything and everything that exists.

As a result, it is impossible for the God of Jewish monotheism to be to rendered in visual images or reduced to the depictions of human-like exploits.

This idea has been at the core of Jewish religious thought from the beginning. But, like water for fish, it is so much part of our religious environment for our entire life that we might lose the ability to even recognize it. Stepping back from or own tradition, defamiliarizing ourselves with it, looking at it in an unfamiliar context, gives us the opportunity to see it afresh. Having "visited" India, we might be able to appreciate more fully the lessons of the Jewish past. One Rabbinic text explores the full meaning of Shema, which is often referred to as "the watchword of our faith:"

> On the verse, "Hear, O Israel, the Lord our God, the Lord is one", the comment is made: The Holy One, blessed be He, said to Israel, "My children, everything that I created in the universe is in pairs…heaven and earth, sun and moon, Adam and Eve… but I am one and alone in the universe.
> (Deuteronomy Rabbah II.31)

This understanding was expressed forcefully by the great Medieval Jewish philosophers. In the traditional prayer book, the morning service begins with the familiar hymn, *Adon Olam*. Maybe we are accustomed to arriving late, or are too busy greeting our fellow worshippers. Or maybe we do not know that what we are singing is really an eleventh century credal formulation. In any event, what is being sung is this very central idea:

> When all [creation] ceases to be
> Still will He reign in awesome majesty
> He is One
> And there is no second that can be compared to Him
> Or associated with Him.

This lesson at the very start of the service asserts explicitly that nothing can be considered remotely like God. And that same lesson is reaffirmed at the conclusion of the service, in the closing hymn, a musical rendition of another Medieval creed, the *Yigdal*, which again teaches, "He is One and unique in His Unity...He has no bodily form and nothing resembling a body." Maimonides brought this religious perspective to its fullest formulation when he taught about the incorporeality of God. "God," he said, "is One, with no unity comparable to His unity." Indeed, he argues that there is nothing that finite human beings can say about the infinite God. The best we can do is talk about what God is not. Indeed, through an ingenious translation, he understands Psalm 65:2 as asserting, "to You, silence is praise." And he admonishes us that the proper way to speak of God is ... silence.

Unlike the Hindu tradition, the Jewish tradition teaches an absolute incorporeality. The God of Jewish tradition is emphatically disembodied. It is possible for us to lose sight of just how radical a vision that is. It leaves little room for visual depiction or narrative rendition. In more recent times, this same idea was taught by the great Jewish thinker Martin Buber, who warns that any attempt to understand God, or reduce God to a formula comprehensible to our finite minds, to say virtually anything at all about God (here he echoes Maimonides), runs the risk of reducing the infinite God to an "idol." He tells a story about a "wise old thinker" who challenges him for even writing about God:

> How can you bring yourself to say "God" time after time? How can you expect that your readers will take the word in the sense in which you wish it to be taken? What you mean by the name "God" is something above all human grasp and comprehension, but in speaking about it you have lowered it to human conceptualization.... When I hear the highest called "god," it sometimes seems almost blasphemous.

To which Buber replies, "certainly [people] draw caricatures and write 'God' underneath." Buber suggests that imagining that our own conception of God somehow captures the reality of God in God's fullness, turns our conception into an idol.

Sometimes we live so closely with people that we lose the ability to see them as they are. So, too, it is possible for the central idea of Jewish monotheism to become so routine for us that we lose sight of its radical implications and of the uniqueness of its vision. By looking respectfully and empathetically at a different religious perspective, we can gain new understanding. We can begin to see the contours of this different religious perspective more clearly, and begin to appreciate its unique place in the vast and varied landscape of human religiousness.

# chapter 3

# Things Change

The previous two chapters are really a pair. They talk about the evolution of the understanding of God in the Jewish tradition (as we moved up our Torah *tel*) and the deepest implications of that understanding when it came into its full flowering in the period after the close of the Torah. And yet, introducing the idea of evolution here might strike some as troubling. We are used to thinking of our Torah as consistent, of a single piece. The idea of biblical religion's changing over time, evolving, is unfamiliar to us, perhaps uncomfortable. And, of course, the Jewish tradition continued to evolve through all the ages of Jewish life in so many different settings. There are people in every religious group who are offended by the suggestion that their religious tradition has evolved. (They may be willing to concede that other traditions evolved, just not their own). For many, the idea that religious traditions evolve seems incongruous. We think of religious traditions as the stuff of eternity. Jews may tend to imagine that our tradition is consistent and homogeneous: the same everywhere and always. But, of course, if we really look at the history of our tradition, it becomes impossible to avoid recognizing in it, as well as in other religious traditions, the significant changes it has undergone as it has moved through time. To see evolution at work in religious traditions, let us start by exploring the striking example of a small, relatively recent, group in India, the Sikhs.

The story of the Sikhs teaches many lessons: the reality that syncretism (one tradition borrowing elements of another) is a significant factor in relations between religious traditions (contrary to our common practice of viewing each of them separately, as if they existed in "silos"); the many, and often unexpected, roles that religious texts play (we will return to this in Chapter 5), and —the subject here—the ways, often unpredictable, that religious traditions transform over time.

The story of the Sikhs begins in 15th- century India, at a time when the Hindu majority country was ruled by a Muslim minority. As we saw in the last chapter, image worship was an important element of Hindu religiousness. The Muslim tradition, on the other hand, was radically and militantly iconoclastic. In other words, Hindus treasured their images, Muslims despised them. And, being in authority, Muslims took the opportunity to deface and destroy religious images wherever they could. And Muslim authorities were harsh with non-Muslims in many other ways as well. As a consequence, there was a great deal of tension, violence, and hatred between the two groups. This became one of those, all-too-frequent, tragic moments in history when religious animosities led to human suffering and death.

Out of these unhappy circumstances emerged a guru (teacher) named Nanak in the Punjab region of northwest India. Guru Nanak preached respect and mutuality. His teaching was epitomized in his assertion, "there is neither Muslim nor Hindu...God is neither Muslim nor Hindu [I will follow the path of God]." Over the years he attracted both Muslims and Hindus to him, creating an oasis from the turmoil of the surrounding society where members of the two groups could live harmoniously. A story told about the end of his life is an embodiment of the message he delivered throughout his career. As Nanak lay dying, his Hindu followers argued that, following Hindu custom, his body ought to be cremated. His Muslim followers, in accord with their tradition, advocated burial. Nanak resolved the issue. "Let Hindus place flowers on one side of my body, and Muslims, the other. In the morning whichever group's flowers remain fresh shall decide how my body is to be disposed of." As his followers sang hymns, he covered himself with a sheet. In the morning, when the sheet was removed, no body was to be found. But the sets of flowers on both sides of the bed were discovered to have remained fresh. The story expresses Nanak's teaching that he was following the path of God, neither Hindu nor Muslim. And it embodies the underlying goal of his project: reconciliation; bridging differences between groups; promoting peace.

This commitment to building bridges is continued in the religious tradition that emerged from his teaching. It is one which incorporated elements of both traditions. Like the other religious traditions of India, Sikhs believe in reincarnation, *dharma, karma,* and liberation from the wheel of rebirth. Like Muslims everywhere they are monotheists, believing rigorously in God's oneness. The Sikh tradition was established in the interests of peace. Its existence, in theory, might be expected to stand as an embodiment of that goal.

Nanak's syncretism represented his effort to achieve intergroup harmony. It was a remarkably pacifistic enterprise. What evolved from it was the creation of yet another religious group in India, one with its own identity and its own self-interest. Over the next two centuries, Nanak was followed by nine successive Gurus. Each was charged with protecting the welfare of the Sikh community. The sixth Guru, Har Gobind—less than a century after Nanak—took to wearing two swords, signifying that he wielded both religious and political authority. But the final transformation of this community—founded to embody pacifist ideals—came later.

Gobind Singh was the last of the Gurus. He had every reason to be anxious, being the successor of Guru Tegh Bahadur, who died at Muslim hands after being imprisoned and tortured for protesting against the Muslim emperor's abuse of non-Muslims in his domain. The story told about Gobind Singh is stunningly different from the story told about the death of Nanak. After elaborate preparation, Guru Gobind Singh summoned his followers to an important gathering. Standing on a raised dais in front of a large tent, he shocked his followers by calling for a volunteer to offer his head as a sacrifice to God. One fervent follower stepped forward and was ushered into the tent, where Gobind Singh had hidden some goats. When he emerged from the tent with a sword dripping with the blood of a goat, the Guru demanded another head, and another, until five of his most faithful followers appeared to the crowd to have been offered up. At the conclusion of this charade, the five "dead" followers emerged from the tent along with the Guru himself, wearing identical clothing as the guru and brandishing gleaming new swords. The lesson, Gobind Singh taught, was that from that moment on Sikhs would be a fighting force committed to defending themselves against their enemies and forcefully attacking opponents. The Sikh community was to be characterized by the sword. Indeed, to this day, all male Sikhs wear a *kirpa*, a symbolic dagger, as testimony to their membership in the community. The name Singh has become a common one among Sikhs. It means lion, an expression of the ferocity Gobind Singh wanted to instill in the community.

In the centuries since Gobind Singh, Sikhs have gained renown as fierce warriors. When the British Empire ruled India, it made use of skilled Sikhs to maintain order and deployed Sikh units in its various wars. Since India achieved its independence, Sikh officers have found themselves among the highest leadership of the Indian military. The history of the Sikhs represents a stunning transformation from a community created for the promotion of peace to one famed for its military prowess. Not all traditions change this dramatically. But all traditions change.

And we need to recognize that the transformation of the Sikhs is not the only example of what we can call paradoxical evolution. The evolution that might be most familiar to us in the West is that of the Christian community (I know that this takes us away from India, but it is just too salient to ignore). In that tradition Jesus, frequently referred to as the Prince of Peace (in appropriation of what the early Church saw as a prophecy in Isaiah 9:6) became the foundation upon which the edifice of the Christian tradition was erected. In the Gospels, Jesus is depicted as teaching lessons of peace and forbearance ("If someone strikes you on the right cheek, turn the other cheek to him as well"). It is easy to see him, like Nanak, as an exponent of pacifism. And yet, ten centuries after Jesus, the head of the now large and powerful Christian Church, Pope Urban II recruited and personally led soldiers bearing the sign of the cross on their shields to wage war—called the Crusades—against the "infidels" in the same "Holy Land" where Jesus had preached his message of peace. And, of course, many of us are familiar with the Christian hymn that enjoins, "Onward, Christian soldiers, marching as to war." One cannot help wondering what Jesus would have made of this. One answer is offered in Dostoevsky's *The Grand Inquisitor*. If you have not read it, I recommend it enthusiastically as a sardonic commentary on the very subject of the evolution of a religious tradition. I mention this not in censure, but to highlight change. And the child is not always father to the man. As with the distance travelled from Nanak to Gobind Singh, the road was a remarkably long one; one that nobody hearing the message of the founder could have predicted. Religious traditions evolve—and often in ways that could never have been predicted at their infancy.

After that brief detour to the West, our last example of the often unpredictable evolution of religious traditions takes us back to India, to explore the teachings of the Buddha (Buddha is not a name, as Christ is not a name. Buddha is an honorific title meaning "the Enlightened One." Christ, by the way, is Greek for messiah/anointed one). In place of looking at the Buddha's teachings, we will look at its application by his followers. The tradition that grew out of his teachings offers us another opportunity to watch the phenomenon of paradoxical evolution. Most people associate the Buddhist tradition with Japan, or China, or other parts of East Asia. But it had its origin in India. In fact, in its beginnings it was a kind of reaction against the dominant religious teachings of its time and place.

The Buddha was the son of a king in the fifth century BCE in what is today Nepal. He renounced his royal life to become a wandering teacher. He was moved to liberate all suffering beings from the pains they endure in their many rebirths. The lesson he taught was far different from the lessons of the Hindu teachers of his time. While they emphasized the constellation of reincarnation, *dharma, karma,* and liberation after many lifetimes, the Buddha promised people that they could achieve *nirvana*—be liberated from the suffering that characterizes human life—in this lifetime … if they followed his example and his prescription. We will have the opportunity to look more closely at the Buddha's lesson in the next chapter. What we will explore here is the way the very form of Buddhist practice changed over time.

The Buddha saw himself as a physician, offering a prescription for people to liberate themselves from human suffering. Unlike the Hindu teachers of his time, he dismissed the caste system and the notion of specific dharmas for each caste and life-stage. His remedy was one that was available to all people, regardless of their station in life. The prescription he offered to all people was the call to engage in deep meditation, which would bring them to enlightenment: profound perspective and an understanding of their true place in the cosmos. His "eight-fold path" to liberation was one each person could tread by themselves, indeed could tread only on their own. (I am reminded of the old song that says, "You've got to cross that lonesome valley, you've got to cross it by yourself. There ain't no one can walk it for you. You've got to walk it by yourself.")

The Buddha's prescription was one of what we today would call "self-healing." If you examine it, you cannot help but notice that it lacked the elements we are used to associating with religion. It featured no religious authorities or leaders, no hierarchy. It did not hearken to any common past or invoke traditions; it offered no particular sacred place. It contains no scripture or sacred texts. It dismissed rituals, included no set of practices: it gave its followers no requirement other than meditation itself. Most strikingly, there was no role in the Buddha's prescription for the supernatural: no gods, no heavenly beings to help suffering souls in the course they had to pursue by themselves to achieve liberation.

One might even regard the Buddha's teaching as essentially a psychology—a means of changing a person's life by changing the way they thought about it. This is so much the case that we could be forgiven for wondering why we even discuss the Buddha's teachings under the rubric of religion rather than study it in the context of psychology or treat it as an ancient therapeutic practice.

And yet, we are confronted with a quandary. The various forms of the Buddhist tradition that we might encounter when we look to Asia somehow do not correspond to this simple teaching of meditation as a prescription for self-liberation. What we see, instead, are magnificent shrines and temples with splendid images of the Buddha wonderfully ornamented or gilded. When we visit these temples, we are more than likely to find people worshipping in front of an image of the Buddha, perhaps making an offering. Indeed, the Buddha himself has come to be treated as a deity who is reverenced and about whom miraculous stories are told. And, more importantly, he is understood to be still available to aid us in our quest for liberation. And he is associated with a supernatural pantheon of divine beings, the identities of whom will vary among Buddhist countries and sub-groups. In many Buddhist traditions, we can also appeal to an array of supernatural beings called *Boddhisattvas,* beings who could themselves enter *nirvana* but have elected, instead, to remain in the world to assist other people in their efforts to be liberated.

Beyond this, there is a panoply of Buddhist phenomena: sacred spaces, such as temples, shrines, images; sacred personalities, religious specialists, hierarchies, and organizations; sacred time, an array of Buddhist holidays, and practices which characterize each of the various forms of Buddhist life; libraries of texts; compelling works of art in many media and styles; songs, prayers and chants. In other words, the "therapeutic" teachings of the Buddha have evolved into a family of traditions that include all the elements of what can only be called religion.

How did this transformation occur? The answer, once again, is history. Not long after the Buddha left this earthly life, the movement that had grown up around him split. One group was, and largely remains to this day, more rigorously attached to the specific teachings and modes of the Buddha himself. It felt that the Buddha's lessons were intended essentially for those who were prepared to devote themselves exclusively to meditation and the quest for liberation: monks. The other group felt that the message of the Buddha was for everyone, monk and lay person alike: for those who could devote themselves exclusively to the quest, and for those whose lives were more caught up with the things of this world, people who might need some additional, supernatural, help in achieving the common goal. The first group put its emphasis on knowledge and saw the Buddha as a saint and a supreme sage. But when he left this world any personal role for him was finished. The second group put its emphasis on compassion and saw the Buddha, motivated by his compassion for all suffering beings, as a world savior who continues to be present, drawing others to him.

In addition, within a few centuries of the death of the Buddha, emissaries were sent to countries throughout Asia, bearing his teaching to new audiences. As Buddhist teaching was planted in new soil, it hybridized. It took on the coloration of the local culture and elements of the local religious tradition (syncretism again!). Which is why the Buddhist traditions of various countries, while they share the same common core, on the surface, look more like the indigenous religious traditions of their respective countries than they resemble each other. Geographic dispersal and a recognition of the needs of different temperaments transformed the prescription of a wandering teacher with a handful of followers into a widespread and variegated tradition that is today embraced by hundreds of millions of people.

What today we could call the family of Buddhist traditions has, like the Sikh tradition, experienced quite a long journey. It has evolved from a non-theistic prescription for self-liberation to a collection of traditions that involves all the elements we associate with religion: including divine and supernatural beings, not the least of whom is the Buddha himself. None of this could have been predicted or extrapolated from the teachings that the first group of disciples learned from the humble wanderer who taught his lessons in India 25 centuries ago.

There is no religious tradition that has not evolved. Whether the fact is comforting or vexing to us, we should not expect that Jewish tradition would be exempt. When Jews reflect on the evolution that has marked the journey of other traditions, they can recognize that Jewish religiousness, too, has evolved over many centuries—and continues to evolve. Though the fact of the evolution of any tradition can be discomfiting—and the experience of it uncomfortable—for its followers, it is an inevitable part of the nature of all religious traditions. In the first chapter, we saw the very understanding of the nature of God evolve from henotheism to monotheism. And in the second chapter, we saw that monotheism blossom into one in which Jewish monotheism became not just a matter of numbers, but of type. God was more than numerically One. God had come to be understood as unique, singular, radically unlike anything else that existed.

Jews who look at their history recognize that the Jewish life of the rabbis in Babylonia was very different from the Jewish life of the Pharisees and Sadducees of the second Temple period. And the life of even the most pious Jew of 19th-century Eastern Europe was far removed from those of the rabbis in Babylonia. Yes, of course, there has been continuity. So many elements of the Jewish past are maintained in the Jewish present, even if in rather different form.

But the nature of Jewish religiousness, as the religiousness of all groups, was one of continuity within ongoing transformation. From worship expressed through a service of sacrifice, to a worship of words offered in prayer; from the religious ministrations of priests, to the teaching and preaching of rabbis; from the portable tabernacle of the wilderness period to the glorious Temple in Jerusalem to the humble *shtieblach* of the shtetl to whatever form Jewish life will take as Jewish religion and culture evolve in the reborn Jewish state in Israel, Jewish religiousness has always been a work in progress. That makes it a living tradition.

# chapter 4

# The Buddha Resolves a Biblical Enigma

We met the Buddha briefly in the last chapter. Now we will have the opportunity to spend some more time with him, and explore his teaching more closely. Because he holds the key to understanding one of the most puzzling books in our whole Tanakh: Torah (the five books of Moses), Prophets (*Nevi'im*), and Writings (*Ktuvim*), which comprise the Hebrew Bible.

Jews think of themselves as the "people of the book." This designation was given to us by Muhammad in recognition of the fact that we are a religious group whose tradition stands on a sacred text. But, truth be told, the fact that we are "of the book" does not mean that we necessarily read the book. There are whole parts of our own scripture that are virtually unknown to us—even to the most learned. Who among us has ever read the book of Daniel? I don't mean who has mastered all of its intricacies, I mean who ever reads it? Or Nehemiah? Or Chronicles? They are in our sacred text. But we do not open them. Whole parts of our spiritual inheritance are uncharted territory to us. And it is not because we are all ill-learned or religiously lax. The truth is that the rabbis who fashioned our religious tradition structured it in such a way that these books, and others, are functionally left out of lived Jewish life.

And even some of those that are part of ongoing Jewish life are still essentially hard for us to make sense of. Ezekiel is perpetually mystifying. The minor prophets are hard for us to make sense of unless our rabbis carefully explain the text to us. Most Jews who hear the snatches of the prophets, which are the Haftarot included in our worship services, appear to lose focus as they are being read.

We regard them as sacred, but they do not make sense to us.

And then there are the selections from the third section of the Tanakh, *Ktuvim*, that the rabbis assigned to the various holidays. Each Pesach we can revel in the beauty of *Shir HaShirim*/The Song of Songs, even if its full meaning eludes us, and even though we can wonder why it was included in the canon to begin with. (There is precedent for our perplexity. The rabbis who assembled the canon debated long and hard about whether this particular book should be included or discarded as many other texts apparently were. Rabbi Akiba, on the other hand, praised it, calling it *Kodesh HaKodashim*/the Holy of Holies.) For the record, the rabbis finally decided to include it because they saw it as a metaphor for God's love of His people.

At Shavuot we are warmed by the sweetness of Ruth's character and of her story. We are moved by the tale even if parts of the narrative are confusing to us. But it is at *Succot* that the assigned reading leaves us completely perplexed. Just what is *Koheleth*/Ecclesiastes and what is it supposed to teach us?

## The Enigma of Koheleth

Appropriately enough, scholars cannot even agree on the precise meaning of the name of the book. It is based on the Hebrew three-letter root KHL, which has the sense of gathering. Thus, the name can suggest that the book represents someone preaching to a *kahal*—a gathering. Or it could suggest that the author was himself a gatherer of wisdom, insights, or aphorisms. Or it could convey the idea that this book itself is a gathering of such insights and lessons. But far more perplexing than this, and far more consequential, is the confusion caused by the very contents of the book.

The ideas put forth in *Koheleth* are not simply different from anything else taught in the Tanakh; they are often radically at odds with it. Things that are important in other parts of the Tanakh are not mentioned in *Koheleth* at all: Shabbat; sacrifices; the Temple;

holidays; the very notion of commandment. All these things, so central elsewhere in the Tanakh, do not appear in this text at all. Similarly absent is any mention of the history of the Jewish people which, of course, is at the very heart of the rest of the biblical text. It is as if this book were a product of a completely different culture.

Even more confounding, *Koheleth* explicitly denies ideas and beliefs that are central to the ideology of the rest of the Tanakh. The rest of the Tanakh speaks about God with a kind of clarity and certainty. Indeed, many sections of the book depict God in the process of self-disclosure through revelation. People can speak about God and God's will because God has shared this knowledge with them. In *Koheleth,* neither revelation nor reason seem to be able to make God or God's will knowable to human beings. It does not seem to take account of revelation, so central in the rest of the text, at all. The pursuit of justice and righteousness is a theme that runs in various ways throughout the rest of the Bible. *Koheleth* calls the very concept of justice into question, indeed counsels against being overzealous in its pursuit: advice inconceivable in the rest of biblical teaching.

*Koheleth* can be disturbing. Its ethic is radically different from what we find in the rest of the Bible. Rather than counselling engagement, it appears to teach caution, aloofness, withdrawal. The dissonance from the rest of the Bible that is true of the ethics of the book is true, as well, of its mood. While the rest of the Tanakh seems to radiate with hope, the tone of *Koheleth* seems to verge on despair.

Commentators and scholars have struggled to make sense of the book, offering many and various interpretations. Some have seen—and dismissed—it as a book of simple hedonism, suggesting that all we can do is enjoy the pleasures of life: "eat, drink and be merry." To others, it is a book of pessimism written by one who has seen the world and all its foolishness and who holds no hope for its improvement; such that, in effect, the author dismisses it as worthless. *Koheleth* has been read as a book of boredom, the musing of a man who has seen and done everything. He is jaded. There is nothing new, nothing left for him; so he dismisses it all as so much "vanity." Some have read it as a book of bitterness. For them it is the text of an old man whose youth and vitality have passed. He is angered that the life he has known is no longer available to him, so he denounces youth as being fleeting. He condemns the past for being evanescent. Still others characterize *Koheleth* as a book of resignation: in the end everything is fated and cannot be changed. All we can do is accept our lot. To still others, *Koheleth* is the record of a quest, the memoir of one who has tried to find ultimate meaning in the enjoyment of wealth and pleasure, in wisdom, and in the pursuit of justice; and found all of these wanting. Nihilism, hedonism, pessimism, boredom, or disillusionment. How can we make sense of a book with such widely different interpretations? The more important question for us must be, is there any way we can find a message in *Koheleth* that is useful in our own lives?

Interestingly, numbers of scholars have sought to understand *Koheleth* by placing it in the context of another culture: Greek philosophy. Some identify it with Stoicism, others with Epicureanism. It has been interpreted in the light of determinism. I agree that *Koheleth* is best understood by looking at it from the perspective of another culture. But I suggest that the best vantage point from which to find a consistent message in this book is the life and teaching of the Buddha. From this perspective *Koheleth* can be seen as a book neither of unbridled hedonism nor of pessimism. Rather, it threads a middle way between these two extremes. It seems to espouse a very clear perspective, albeit one found nowhere else in the Bible.

To be clear, I am not suggesting that the author of *Koheleth* journeyed to India to study and brought this new understanding back home with him; nor that Buddhist monks made their way to Judea to impart their learning to the wisdom teachers there as they did in Asia. And I am not arguing that *Koheleth* and the Buddha speak in a single voice. What I do maintain is that a familiarity with the Buddhist tradition makes it possible for us to approach this unique book of the Bible with a greater clarity. I believe that there is a significant resonance between the two if we are attuned to listening for it. And I am suggesting that our reading of *Koheleth* can be enriched by reading it in the context of this Indian tradition, by understanding it, by analogy, with ideas propounded in Buddhist tradition. Once we read it against this background, it makes a different kind of sense.

## The Life of the Buddha

Now we finally return to the Buddha. We met him briefly in the last chapter, noting there that, while many people believe that Buddha was a person's name, it is actually an honorific title, meaning "the Enlightened One." His given name was Siddhartha, which means "wish-fulfilling." He is often referred to as the Sakyamuni, which means sage of the Sakya clan. Siddhartha Gautama was born in 563 BCE, during the time that the philosopher Karl Jaspers has called the "axial age." The Buddha's contemporaries during that unparalleled moment in human history were Confucius and Lao Tzu in China, Socrates in Greece, Zarathustra in Persia, and Amos, Isaiah, and Jeremiah in Israel. His father was ruler of the clan's kingdom in the northwest part of the Indian subcontinent, in what is today Nepal.

Stories (perhaps mythical, in the sense that students of religion use the term) are told about events surrounding the Buddha's birth, as they are about the births of other significant religious figures: Moses comes to mind in the Torah, or Samson; or Jesus in the Christian tradition. It is said that, soon after the child was conceived, the royal father-to-be summoned the court sages, who predicted that the son who was to be born would be either an omniscient buddha and world liberator, or a world ruler. As might be expected, the father wanted the son to become a world ruler. We might assume that his preference was driven by family tradition, or the desire, common among fathers, to have his son follow in his footsteps. The earliest hearers of the story probably recognized in the father's wishes the extent to which he was motivated by the demands of the prevalent Indian commitment to the concept of *dharma*. Siddhartha, as a member of the *kshatriya*/ruler and warrior caste, would be expected to fulfill that, and only that, role. Enlightenment and world liberating was for *Brahmins*/teachers, the highest caste. Taking on the *dharma* of another could only have unhappy consequences.

The sages admonished the Buddha's father that if his son were to see four specific things, he would abandon his throne—and his *dharmic* duty—and opt for the teacher's role. In examining those things, we recognize three of them as familiar expressions of the suffering that is the human lot, along with one that has profound significance for the path that the Buddha would ultimately follow. They are: old age; sickness; and death; as well as the self-imposed deprivation and suffering of the wandering ascetic.

The Buddha's father, not wanting his son to see the sights that would lead him away from his royal life, conspired to prevent his son from seeing any of these "four sights." He created an artificial world for him, a "pleasure palace" that he was not allowed to leave. He insured that all the worldly distractions that could be provided of a young man were lavished on him. He was supplied with the best of food, artistic surroundings, music, and company. He was surrounded only by beautiful, healthy, young people. Those who fell ill or who aged out were removed from the young Siddhartha's environment. At sixteen, he was married to the most beautiful young woman in the kingdom, his cousin, Yasodhara. Very soon she bore him a son, named, symbolically enough, Rahula, literally "bond" or "link," in testimony to his grandfather's wish that he would be the link that held the Buddha to the life of the palace, that held him fast to that artificial world.

But things did not work out as the king hoped. Something stirred within Siddhartha. Perhaps he intuited the unnaturalness of his situation. Something inside him made him long to see the world outside his pleasure palace. He bribed his charioteer to take him outside the walls of his home. When he left the grounds of the palace, he saw things he had never seen before, indeed had never even heard of. On that first illicit trip outside the palace walls, Siddhartha saw a person worn down by age. That sight must have shocked the young prince. Undoubtedly, he pondered it and sought some explanation for it as he was returned to the palace. Clearly, he was moved by what he had seen and wished to learn more. He arranged for further visits outside his circumscribed world. On successive excursions, he saw a person racked by disease; the body of a dead person; and then an ascetic recluse—a man who had sought to overcome these very three miseries of human experience by immersing himself in the practice of asceticism and self-denial—long common in Indian culture.

The result of seeing those four sights was every bit as destabilizing as the royal sages had predicted. Those visits outside the walls of the palace led the young prince to change the course of his life; and, as a result, the course of so much of the world was changed forever. Siddhartha had the profound insight that drove him to fulfill the sages' prediction. Moved by compassion for the suffering he had witnessed, he resolved to leave the palace for good and to devote himself to bringing healing to the world—liberation from the suffering that he had come to understand was the stuff of human life. One night he left the palace for the final time. In the Buddhist world, that event is called "the night of the great going forth." On that night he gave up everything that was his, everything he had known. He broke the bond. He left his son and his wife and abandoned the life of the pleasure palace forever. Like Abraham in Genesis, he literally left his "land ... [his] birthplace, and ... [

his] father's house." He abandoned the kingship and worldly rule and set out to learn how he could liberate the world from all its suffering.

Siddhartha began his journey by going to seek out the forest-dwelling philosophers who were plentiful enough in the India of his day. After spending significant time with them, he decided that philosophy had nothing to offer in answering the problem of human suffering. He joined a group of austere ascetics who indulged in the most rigorous kinds of self-denial and self-punishment. Asceticism was a widely practiced expression of Indian religion. One contemporary of the Buddha named Mahavira, who went on to found the Jain tradition, is described as going about naked, inviting insects to afflict his body, barely eating or drinking; in the coldest times intentionally seeking out the shadiest spot to meditate in; and in summer finding the place for his meditation that was most exposed to the sun. It is taught that the Buddha became a master of such ascetic practice, winning the admiration of a group of other ascetics to which he had become attached, going days without eating or drinking. Buddhist tradition has it that he lived a life of extreme austerity for seven years. Finally, after depriving himself of all food or drink for an extended period of time, he fell into a stupor. Upon awakening, it is said, he came to the recognition that the ascetic path, rather than leading to enlightenment, simply led to more suffering. He abandoned the course of renunciation and self-mortification ... as well as the five ascetics with whom he had joined, who proceeded to denounce him for abandoning the righteous life.

Having been disappointed by hedonism, wisdom, and, now, asceticism, he sought a different way. It was then that one of the great transformational moments in religious history took place. Siddhartha found his way to a place that came to be called Bodh Gaya in Bihar in northeastern India. There he sat under a particular tree: now known to Buddhists as the Bo tree, the tree of enlightenment.

For seven weeks, he devoted himself to intense meditation. At the conclusion of those forty-nine days he achieved his own great awakening: the enlightenment he pursued with such resolution. Siddhartha Gautama had become the Buddha.

Upon achieving enlightenment, the Buddha began his life's work of proclaiming his lessons to all who would listen. He travelled to the already-sacred city of Benares; and, in an area known as the Deer Park, he delivered his first teaching. As fate would have it, the five ascetics whose company he had abandoned earlier also happened to be in the Deer Park, and, upon seeing him, decided to stay and jeer. Instead, they found themselves moved and convinced by his teaching and became his disciples, the first members of the *sangha*: his order of male and female monks who would accompany him for the rest of his life.

## The Buddha's Message

In a way, the heart of the Buddha's message is anticipated in the "four sights" that he came to see despite his father's best efforts to shield him from them. In Buddhist tradition, as in Jewish tradition, important ideas are often transmitted through stories that are usually considerably less simple than they appear. One such story about the Buddha concerns a woman whose child had died. Distraught, she wandered from place to place carrying the body of her child, hoping to find someone who could restore her lost son to her. Teacher after teacher dismissed her, unable to provide her the help she needed. Finally, she sought out the Buddha. Unlike the others, he told her that, yes, he certainly could revive her son—if she could bring him a handful of mustard seeds from a household that had never been touched by death. And so the bereaved mother set out, going from house to house begging for mustard seeds. And at every house she was told of death of a family member. Death turned out to be a universal human experience. Everyone suffers loss. To be human is to suffer.

As he demonstrated when he left the forest-dwelling philoso-phers, the Buddha did not see himself as a philosopher or theore-tician. Rather, he sought a cure for the reality of human loss and suffering. He described himself as a physician. He was not con-cerned with examining or explaining the workings of the cosmos. Instead, he felt a compelling desire to help people overcome the painful realities of their lives.

The analogy he used was of coming upon someone who had been shot with an arrow. You do not begin by discussing archery with them. You don't engage them in a conversation about the nature of the arrow with which they have been pierced: what kind of wood was the shaft made of? What kind of feathers did it have? You don't discuss the circumstances of the shooting either: who do you think shot you? Why did they shoot you? Where do you think they were standing when they shot you? Instead, you pull the arrow out (although current first aid protocols advise against this) and set about healing the wound. So it is with the human condition. His goal, he said, was not to help people understand the world, but to help them deal with the pain that comes from living in it.

So we return to the Deer Park in Benares to stand with the Bud-dha's first disciples as he delivers that first lesson. It expresses the very core of what would become the Buddhist tradition with all its variations and permutations. The Buddha's fundamental lesson is called the "chain of dependent origination." Each human being, he teaches, is caught up on the wheel of *samsara*—the endless cycle of life, death and rebirth. We are held on that wheel by *karma*: the consequences of our actions in each life. To this point the message of the Buddha is no different from other Indian teachings: the notion that what we do affects what becomes of us as we return, unendingly, to this world. What is unique in the Buddha's lesson is that he proposes a remedy to this situation. He offers a way to leave the wheel of *samsara*—in this lifetime. The Buddha called the first of his teachings "the four noble truths."

The first noble truth is the truth of *dukkha*. All life is *dukkha*. The word *dukkha* is often translated as suffering. And it does include the intense pain that we associate with that term. But it also includes the more low-level sense we have that things are just not right, are awry, out of kilter, askew. *Dukkha* might even be understood as the opposite of the (occasional and fleeting) sense of well-being that we can experience. Perhaps *dukkha* is that sense of ill-being we so often have. Everything is not all right. The world is out of joint. All of life is suffused with the realities that Siddhartha saw, and the emotions he must have felt, when he slipped out of the palace those four times: the pain aroused by the disjointedness of old age, sickness, and death (our pain at the loss of loved ones, our fear of it for ourselves), or what the distraught mother experienced trying to find a household whose members had been unscathed by death. This, says the Buddha, is the ground reality of human life.

The Buddha's second lesson is about cause and effect. Things have a cause. *Dukkha* has a cause, and that cause is *tanha,* the craving that constantly gnaws at us. We want things; we crave things; we grasp for things. Or at least we want to hold onto things, keep the things we love permanent: and that can never be. *Tanha* is responsible for the disjointedness in our lives. We want what we don't have. And then, when we have it, as Irving Berlin wrote, "After you get what you want, you don't want it." And we want something else. Or, if we are satisfied with it, we want more. Endlessly. Pay attention to your own words. Listen to how many times a day, and in how many contexts, you use the phrase, "I want." We want…. And so, we are always in the throes of *tanha* and thus suffer *dukkha*.

The third noble truth is an extrapolation from the second: to overcome *dukkha*, you must overcome *tanha*. Conquering your craving, your endless wanting, frees you from the gnawings of *dukkha*.

At this point let us note that the first three noble truths read like a physician's diagnosis. The physician determines what is wrong—

craving—and identifies the cause of craving. The physician also identifies the cure, which is simply to cease craving. It is in the fourth noble truth that the Buddha prescribes a remedy.

The fourth noble truth teaches us that the way to cease craving is to follow a specific set of behaviors. The Buddha called it the "eightfold path"—specific actions that will lead to the end of craving. What you have to do is to cease wanting, to overcome the acquisitive instinct and the grasping part of yourself. And to accomplish this there is a clear formula. Have right thought: know the four noble truths. Free yourself from lust, ill will, and cruelty. Do not lie, do not engage in tale-bearing. Engage in right action; abstain from killing, stealing, or improper sexual relations. Pursue a right livelihood. Engage in right effort. Aspire to right mindfulness and right concentration. If you master that path, the Buddha taught, you will cease your *tanha*, your craving. You will overcome your wanting, and you will free yourself from *dukkha*. That is the heart of the Buddha's teaching. All that was to become the Buddhist tradition grew from this.

At the core of the Buddha's teaching is the lesson that, when you are able to cease grasping, to let go, you are freed from the wheel of *samsara*. You will have arrived at *nirvana*. Many people labor under the misconception that nirvana is some kind of paradise, similar to the Western image of heaven. The reality is that *nirvana* literally means "going out" as a flame goes out when you blow on it. *Nirvana* is a kind of cessation, like what happens to the flowing water when you turn off the faucet. *Nirvana* is the goal of following the eightfold path. It is the end product of our ceasing to crave, of our ceasing to be driven by our wants for things of this world.

Living according to the Buddha's prescription enables us to walk what he called the middle way. We live between the extremes of the indulgence of the senses that he, himself, had known before he left the palace, and the world-renunciation and self-mortification that he experienced while he pursued the life of an ascetic. You do not have to inflict pain on yourself: to do what many of the holy men of the Buddha's time did, like walk on hot coals, lie on a bed of nails, or starve yourself. This, he taught, was just another kind of *dukkha*. In directing us toward the middle way, the Buddha did not advocate the mortification of the flesh that characterizes the life of the ascetic, nor did he teach the disengagement from the world that characterizes the life of a hermit. He did not promote a cult of death or physical self-extinction. Suicide is not his solution to the problem of craving.

The essence of the Buddha's solution is not moving out of life, but the perspective with which we approach the life we live. For the Buddha, mastery comes, finally, in conducting our lives free from attachment to the stuff of our lives. Our material selves go on. Our bodies have their own momentum, and we cannot cause that functioning to stop. What we can do is master our psychological framing of those actions. The Buddha would have us live with our actions—in detachment from their results. We do what must be done, mentally liberated from those actions and from the fruit of those actions. He called this "disinterested action."

As it happens, the notion of disinterested action was not new with the Buddha. His teaching reflects one particular strain of Indian thought that was also presented in one of the fundamental texts of the Hindu tradition, perhaps its most beloved book, the Bhagavad Gita. There it is presented with greater elaboration. Looking at the Gita can help us understand more clearly this aspect of the Buddha's teaching:

> Let your interest be on action alone
> Never on its fruits
> Let not the fruits of action be your motive
> Nor be attached to inaction
> Remaining disciplined
> Abandoning attachment...

Being indifferent to success or failure;
Discipline is defined as indifference.

(Bhagavad Gita II 47–48)

Always unattached
Perform action that must be done
by performing action without attachment
Man attains the highest.

(Bhagavad Gita III.19)

Fools, attached to action
As they act...
So the wise man should act (but) unattached.

(Bhagavad Gita III.24)

These verses from the Bhagavad Gita, express, perhaps more clearly, the same lesson that the Buddha propounded. They cannot be understood to advocate inactivity or passivity. To live requires that we act. It does not require that we become emotionally invested in those actions, or in their results.

The Buddha did not go about naked. He wore clothes to keep his body warm and protected. He ate food and he drank. He would sit in the shade in the summer and find a warm place to meditate in the winter. This became the practice of his followers as well. To this day, Buddhist monks leave their monasteries to go about with their begging bowls to beg for food and drink. They don't beg with specific expectations. Disinterestedly, they take what they are given. They live in pleasant, though not luxurious, residences. They conduct themselves simply as human beings. Indeed, we are taught that when a monk once asked the Buddha what was the right thing for a monk to do, he replied, "Wash your bowls." To live requires that we take care of our bodies, and that we take various actions that are required of us by the circumstances of our lives. No reason to starve yourself. No reason to eat out of filthy bowls. Wash your bowls.

What the verses from the Gita, and the lessons of the Buddha, teach, is to act without emotional engagement with the results of our action. It is the acting itself that is significant. They teach us to abandon the "fruits" of that action. Such "disinterested action" allows human beings to carry on with their lives, freed from the bonds of craving. It allows us to live in the world without being ensnared by it. The Buddha's lesson does not call us out of life, but presents us with a psychology of living a life that transcends the obsessive fixations that flow from the constant pull of *tanha*.

## Koheleth read in light of the Buddha

We turn, finally, from the life and teaching of the Buddha to the enigmatic text of *Koheleth*. We have paid such careful attention to the Buddhist tradition's presentation of the life of the Buddha and of his teachings because reading this biblical text in the light of that background causes its ideas and perspectives to be seen in sharper relief. We see aspects of it that might not have presented themselves to us otherwise. We can perceive patterns of thought in the text and understand this book more sensitively when we read it against what we know of the Buddhist tradition. We might even find a consistent message in this book which is often seen as diffuse and scattered.

## The Life of Solomon

Current biblical scholarship, you should know, is largely in agreement that *Koheleth* was not actually written by King Solomon. Yet the book presents itself as being the work of this illustrious monarch. And reading it in terms of that literary device adds layers of interest and dimensions of meaning for us. The book, as it presents itself to us as the creation of Solomon, invites us to imagine that its author lived the life associated with what we know about the life of King Solomon as it is related to us in the book of I Kings, and also of how he is represented in two other biblical books that also claim to be written by him: The Song of Songs and Proverbs. Both of those books go out of their way to insist on Solomonic authorship. The Song of Songs begins with the words, "The Song of Songs which is of Solomon" (Song of Songs 1:1). The Book of Proverbs underscores Solomon's authorship at several points:

> The Proverbs of Solomon, son of David, King of Israel…
>
> (Proverbs 1:1)

> The proverbs of Solomon…
>
> (Proverbs 10:1)

> These too are proverbs of Solomon, which the men of King Hezekiah of Judah copied.
>
> (Proverbs 25:1)

Remarkably, the outlines of that life run along very similar lines to what we have learned about the life of the Buddha.

What can we say about Solomon? We can imagine him as a pampered prince being raised in the court of his father, King David. We know that he lived quite a luxurious life:

> Solomon's daily provisions consisted of thirty measures of fine flour, and sixty measures of [ordinary] flour, ten fattened oxen, twenty pasture-fed oxen, and one hundred sheep and goats, besides deer and gazelles, roebucks and fatted geese.
>
> (I Kings 5:2–3)

The king made a great throne of ivory and overlaid
it with the finest gold...

And all the king's drinking vessels were of gold
and all the vessels of ... [the royal palace] were of
gold. None were of silver.

(I Kings 10:18 and 21)

He had seven hundred royal wives and three
hundred concubines.

(I Kings 11:3)

It is this hedonistic aspect of Solomon's personality that is
evoked by depicting him as the author of *Shir HaShirim*/The Song
of Songs with all the sensual and erotic elements of the "author's"
life which that suggests:

King Solomon made for himself a palanquin
Of wood from Lebanon
He made its posts of silver
Its back of gold
Its seat of purple wood
Within it was decked with love
By the maidens of Jerusalem
O maidens of Jerusalem go forth
And gaze upon King Solomon....

(Song of Songs 3:9–11)

We also know that Solomon was engaged in the pursuit of wisdom; and that he attained worldwide acclaim for just how wise
he became:

God endowed Solomon with wisdom and dis-
cernment in great measure with understanding

as vast as the sands on the seashore. Solomon's
wisdom was greater than the wisdom of all the
Kedemites and all the wisdom of the Egyptians.
He was the wisest of all men.... His fame spread
among all the surrounding nations. He composed three thousand proverbs and his songs
numbered one thousand and five. He discoursed
about trees, from the cedar of Lebanon to the
hyssop that grows out of the wall; and he discoursed about beasts, birds, creeping things
and fishes. Men of all peoples came to hear Solomon's wisdom, [sent] by all the kings of the
earth who had heard about Solomon's wisdom.
(I Kings 5:9–14)

It is this wisdom that is celebrated in the story of the two
prostitutes who both claim to be the mother of the same baby (I
Kings 3:16–28) and in the narrative about the visit of the Queen
of Sheba who came all the way from her country to Solomon's
court because of "the report I heard in my own land about you
and your wisdom" (I Kings 10:6). Solomon's wisdom is the
reason that the Book of Proverbs is attributed to him.

It is with this picture of Solomon in mind that *Koheleth* has its
author—supposedly Solomon—describe his life in these terms:

I ventured to tempt my flesh with wine and
grasp folly, while letting my mind direct to wisdom, to the end that I might learn which of the
two was better for men to practice in their few
days of life... I multiplied my possessions, I
built myself houses and I planted vineyards. I
laid out gardens and groves, in which I plant
ed every kind of fruit tree. I constructed pools

of water, enough to irrigate forests shooting up
with trees. I bought male and female slaves, and
I acquired stewards. I also acquired more cattle,
both herds and flocks, than all who were before
me in Jerusalem. I further amassed silver and
gold and treasures of kings and provinces; and
I got myself male and female singers, as well as
the luxuries of commoners—coffers and coffers of them. Thus I gained more wealth than
anyone before me in Jerusalem. In addition, my
wisdom remained with me, I withheld from my
eyes nothing they asked for, and denied myself
no enjoyment; rather, I got enjoyment out of
all my wealth.

(Koheleth 2:3–10)

This is how the author of *Koheleth*, whom we might call "Solomon," presents the course of his life. Reading it we cannot help
but be reminded of the life of the young Gautama. Like him, he
was raised in the midst of great luxury. As he grew up, he found
himself surrounded by every kind of pleasure—explicitly in
the case of "Solomon" and by implication in the case of young
Gautama—including an abundance of women.

But for the author of *Koheleth* no less than for the future Buddha, this life of sensual plenty proved to be insufficient:

I said to myself, "Come I will treat you to merriment. Taste mirth!" This, too, I found was futile. Of revelry I said, "it is mad!" of merriment,
"what good is that?"

And, like the Buddha, he decided to devote himself to the
pursuit of knowledge and wisdom:

> All this I tested with wisdom. I thought I could
> fathom it, but it eludes me. [The secret of] what
> happens is elusive[,] and deep, deep down, who
> can discover it? I put my mind to studying, explor-
> ing, and seeking wisdom and the reason of things,
> and to studying wickedness, stupidity, madness
> and folly. Now, I find women more bitter than
> death; she is all traps, her hands are fetters and her
> heart is snares. He who is pleasing to God escapes
> her, and he who is displeasing is caught by her.
> "See, this is what I found", said *Koheleth*, "item by
> item in my search for the reason of things."
>
> (*Koheleth* 7:23–29)

Wisdom in itself not proving to be the solution that either "Solomon" or Gautama had imagined, each of them turned, in differing
ways, to positions that can only be called life-rejecting:

> Then I recounted those who had died long since
> more fortunate than those who are still living; and
> happier than either are those who have not yet
> come into being and have never witnessed the
> miseries that go under the sun.
>
> (*Koheleth* 4:2–3)

> "The day of a man's death is better than the day
> of his birth."
>
> (*Koheleth* 7:1)

> And so I loathed life…
>
> (*Koheleth* 2:17)

Yet truth was not to be found, for either, in the renunciation of life. And so, in the end, each found a middle way between the earlier hedonism of their youth and the world-rejection of later years. "Solomon" as depicted in *Koheleth*, no less than the Buddha, reemerged from his quest reengaged with life, and assumed the role of teacher:

> Because [he] was a sage, he continued to instruct people. He listened to and tested the soundness of many maxims.
>
> *(Koheleth* 12:9)

## Diagnosis: The instability of Human Life

The best way to make sense of *Koheleth* is to read it with Buddhist eyes. *Koheleth* is, as one interpretation of its enigmatic name implies, a collection—a gathering of aphorisms and insights. It has many strands. Reading it against the background of the teachings of the Buddha helps one of those strands stand out in sharper relief. Considered in this light, we can find a *Koheleth* with the thread of a clear and consistent message running through it. That thread makes *Koheleth* a book about *dukkha*. This does not make the book any more conventionally Jewish; but it is the only thread that holds *Koheleth* together. "Solomon" is distressed that life is perpetually out of kilter. Life is never on an even keel, says *Koheleth*. Life cannot be rendered permanent. It is somehow seriously awry. That is the final sense of the Hebrew phrase *havel havalim,* that stands at the very beginning of the book (1:2) and echoes through it.

The leitmotif of the book, in Hebrew, *havel havalim, hacol havel,* is a difficult phrase to translate. The translation we are most familiar with, the King James rendition of the phrase as "vanity of vanities" (not in the sense of primping in front of mirrors, but rather, "in vain"), does not really capture the depth of its meaning.

A better translation is "futility of futilities, all is futility." The best understanding of the phrase comes from dealing with it literally. Etymologically, *havel* is that frozen breath we exhale on a bitter cold winter day. For an instant it hangs before us; then it is gone. That is more than vain or futile. It is evanescent. And so is everything in life. There are no permanent forms. The pre-Socratic Greek philosopher, Heraclitus, taught that you cannot step into the same river twice. In a Buddhist or *Koheleth*-like frame of mind we might say you cannot step into the same river once. The river is never the same. There is no permanence. *Havel havalim*, says *Koheleth*, frost of frost, vapor of vapors: the vaporousness of our very existence. There is nothing substantial in our lives. It is all—we are all—but vapors, insubstantiality. We are, at best, in transit.

In announcing this theme at the very beginning of the book, the author identifies the message that binds together all its seemingly disjointed parts. Running through *Koheleth* is a profound dissatisfaction with all things human and natural. In the course of "Solomon's" explorations, everything turns out to be displeasing. Nothing is ultimately rewarding.

Our strength and powers and health fail us. We fall sick. We grow old. These "three sights," if you will, are what is so mordantly and graphically expressed in the extended metaphor at the beginning of chapter 12:

> Remember then your Creator, in the days of your
>   youth
> Before the evil days come
> And the years draw near when you will say,
> "I have no pleasure in them";
> Before the sun and the light and the moon
> And the stars are darkened,
> And the clouds return after the rain;

In the day when the keepers of the house will
    tremble;
And the strong men shall bow themselves,
And the grinders cease because they are few,
And those that look out shall be darkened in the
    windows,
And the doors shall be shut in the street,
When the sound of the grinding is low;
And one shall be startled at the voice of a bird;
And the daughters of music shall be brought low;
Also when they shall be afraid of that which is high,
And terrors shall be in the way
And the almond-tree shall blossom,
And the grasshopper shall drag itself along,
And the caperberry shall fail;
Because man goes his long way home,
And the mourners go about in the streets;
Before the silver cord is snapped asunder,
and the golden bowl is shattered and the pitcher is
    broken at the fountain,
and the wheel falls shattered into the pit;
and the dust returns to the earth as it was
and the spirit returns to God who gave it.
*Havel havalim…hacol havel.*

(*Koheleth* 12:1–8)

Like much poetry, this metaphor may seem impenetrable. Some
assume that the verses describe the collapse of a house or some
other building. That is probably too literal a reading. And, yes,
many of these verses seem to be written in a code that we cannot
decipher. But clearly these verses are most easily understood as a
collection of various metaphors describing the body's deteriora-
tion as part of the process of aging. Along with verses we cannot

penetrate are some whose meaning is pretty clear. The legs get weak, and the eyes dim. Our hearing fails, and we lose our teeth and so forth. All of which remind us that our life, all of it is *havel*. And then there are those verses at the end, which are not metaphorical at all:

> Man goes his long way home
> And the mourners go about the streets…
> …
> The dust returns to the earth as it was
> And the spirit returns to God who gave it.

Running through *Koheleth* is the awareness of the everpresence of death. Those we love die. And we die. *Koheleth* is preoccupied with this process of loss and with death.

> For that which befalls the sons of men befalls the beasts; the same thing befalls them. As one of them dies, so dies the other. Really, they all have the same breath. So, man has no superiority to the beast. All is *havel.*
>
> (*Koheleth* 3:19)

> This is an evil thing in all that is done under the sun, that there is one event that comes to all. And, yes, the heart of the sons of men is full of evil, and madness is in their heart while they live, and after that they go to the dead…. The dead do not know anything, neither do they have any more reward, for the memory of them is forgotten. Their love, their hatred, their envy has perished long ago. They have no more portion forever in anything that is under the sun.
>
> (*Koheleth* 9:3–6)

Even if they live a thousand years twice over—and
enjoy no good—do not all go to the same place?
(*Koheleth* 6:6)

The day of a man's death
  is better than the day of his birth
It is better to go to the house of mourning
Than to go to the house of feasting;
For that is the [real] end of all men.
(*Koheleth* 7:1–2)

The world about us has no permanence. We can amass great
material wealth, all manner of good things—as Solomon so con-
spicuously did. But we cannot maintain the pursuit forever. Nor
can we forever hold on to all our precious things:

For what will the man be like who will succeed
the one who is "lord" over what he has amassed
long ago. My thoughts also turned to appraising
wisdom and madness and folly. I found that there
is a grievous evil which I have seen under the sun,
namely riches kept by their owner to his hurt, and
those riches happen to perish... As he came forth
from his mother's womb, naked, so will he return
as he came, and he shall take nothing [with him]
for all his hard work that he could carry in his
hand. And this also is a grievous evil, that in the
very way he came in, so shall he go out. And what
does it profit him that he labors for the wind?
(*Koheleth* 5:12–15)

Even the much-vaunted wisdom is not permanent. We can seek
after wisdom, but we cannot hold onto it forever:

Wisdom is better than folly
As light is better than darkness.
A wise man has eyes in his head
Whereas a fool walks in darkness.

But I also found that the same fate awaits them both.
So I reflected, "the fate of the fool is also destined
for me." To what advantage, then, have I been wise?
And I came to the conclusion that that too was
*havel*. Because the wise man, just like the fool, is
not remembered forever. For as succeeding days
roll by, both are forgotten. Alas, the wise man dies,
just like the fool! And so I loathed life. For I was
distressed by all that goes on under the sun. Because
everything is *havel* and a chasing after the wind.

(*Koheleth* 2:2–17)

*Koheleth* is clear in spelling out the source of his discontent. The
origin of his affliction is the lack of permanence in his world. We
can amass material goods. But we cannot go on amassing forever.
We can pursue wisdom, but we do not hold that wisdom forever.
Because, for *Koheleth,* the fundamental discontent is that *we* are
not forever.

So it goes throughout the book. The diagnosis *Koheleth* delivers
to us is the identification of that kind of *havel*—that kind of transito-
riness, that futility. That, for him, is the boundary of all experience.
Here, above all, is where we find the resonance with the teaching of
the Buddha. The discovery for "Solomon" of the *havel* at the root of
all experience has kinship with the Buddha's *dukkha*. For both, the
lessons were triggered by the encounter with sickness, aging, death,
and the distress that flow from them. For both, the startling insight
was that reality cannot be held firm. Our reality is not permanent.
In effect, it is not fully existent. Like frost, it is present temporarily,

but then it is gone. How can we pine after it? What is the sense of craving it? Why be ensnared by *tanha? Dukkha of dukkhas,* says *Koheleth,* all is *dukkha.*

## Prescription:
## Living Life Through Disinterested Action

And yet, of course, if all we can take away from *Koheleth* is a deepened awareness of the transience of all things, how can it be of help to us in living our lives? But *Koheleth,* no less than the Buddha, also offers us a lesson for how to go about living, even with the awareness of the transitory nature of our reality. We are not going to make anything permanent. Things change. Things break. Things and people leave us. We are not going to make anything permanent, so our goal cannot be the achievement of permanence. What, then, should we do with our lives? Why pursue wisdom? Or eat and drink? Why undertake anything at all? Perhaps we should embrace an attitude of complete passivity. Or nihilism. What is the sense of continuing on with our daily existence?

Ultimately, *Koheleth* seems to suggest that the answer to this question is that the very experience of living is valuable in itself: that the simple experiences of our lives have value in, of, and for themselves. The doing of the deeds that make up our daily lives is valuable in itself, not for any imagined permanence that might result from it.

The Buddha (like the Bhagavad Gita) called that kind of attitude to our behavior "disinterested action." We do the actions of our lives for the action's own sake, not because we are attached to the fruit of that action, or because we are waiting for the rewards of the action. We do what we must do because that is what people do; not because we are going to amass a storehouse of wisdom or possessions, or even pleasure. The Buddha taught that there is no way that physical beings can avoid action. Action is inevitable. In teaching the middle way he rejected self-mortification and renunciation. The struggle to oppose what is irresistible is folly. Why waste our efforts on that—that is just another kind of *dukkha*. We do, says, the Buddha, what we must do. Freedom from attachment to what we inevitably—irresistibly—do is the key to our release from suffering. This understanding is epitomized in a paraphrase of the Buddha's own teaching in a well-known Buddhist text, *Questions of King Milinda*: "Without being attached to the body... [enlightened ones] take care of it for the purpose of making a righteous life possible."

That same lesson lies at the heart of *Koheleth*. The first thing "Solomon" would have us look for is tranquility: "Better a hand full of gratification than two fists full of labor, which is chasing after the wind" (*Koheleth* 4:6). (Interestingly, this admonition sounds very much like a verse in another book also said to have been written by Solomon: "Better is a dry crust with peace than a house full of feasting with strife" (Proverbs 17:1). This issue is the subject of the opening verses of chapter 6:

> There is an evil I have observed under the sun,
> and a grave one it is for man; that God sometimes
> grants a man riches, property, and wealth, so that he
> does not want for anything his appetite may crave,
> but God does not permit him to enjoy it; instead
> a stranger will enjoy it. That is *havel* and a grievous
> ill. Even if a man should beget a hundred children
> and live many years—no matter how many the days
> of his years may come to, if his gullet is not satis-
> fied by his wealth, I say: the stillbirth—even if it
> is not accorded a burial—is more fortunate than
> he. Though it comes into *havel* and departs into
> darkness, though it has never seen or experienced
> the sun, it is better off than he. Indeed, even if one
> lived a thousand years twice over but never had his

fill of satisfaction! For are not both of them bound
for the same place? All of man's earning is for the
sake of his mouth. Yet his gullet is never satisfied.
(*Koheleth* 6:1–9)

In *Koheleth's* teaching, the cause of pain is the overwhelming craving that characterizes so much of the human experience. A person
might be rich in material goods, insight, and offspring (as, apparently, Solomon was) and yet be unable to stop wanting. The person
*Koheleth* describes in these verses is driven by *tanha. Koheleth* warns
us that this *tanha* will entrap us and cause us suffering. It were as
if he had issued a warning: "if you keep craving, you will never be
satisfied."

Against this background of the futility of our incessant craving,
*Koheleth* lays out what we must regard as his "middle way:"

There is no good for man (except) that he should eat
and drink and make himself see the good of his toil.
(*Koheleth* 2:24)

I know that there is no good for them (except) that
every man should eat and drink and make himself see
good in all his toil.
(*Koheleth* 3:12–13)

Go your way, eat your bread with joy
And drink your wine with a merry heart…
Whatever your hand finds to do, do that while you
are able. For there is no work, nor reckoning, nor
knowledge, nor wisdom in the grave, to which you go.
(*Koheleth* 9:7–10)

Other verses teach the same lesson. This resembles nothing so much as the Buddhist teachings we have already encountered:

> Without being attached to the body… [enlightened
>     ones] take care of it….
> Wash your bowls.

When we read the Buddhist strand of *Koheleth,* its lesson appears to us as not embittered but descriptive. "Solomon" is here dealing objectively with the reality of death, transience, and loss—not bemoaning it. He understands this as the human condition. *Koheleth* prepares us to recognize that it is the breaking of the cycle of craving that changes the quality of "the days we have under the sun." For we can carry nothing of our wealth away with us. Nor our wisdom.

That same understanding also enables us to recognize, as well, that the lesson of *Koheleth* is not one of empty hedonism. Not for *Koheleth* the sentiments of the Renaissance poem (variously attributed to Ben Jonson or John Fletcher) which so much resembles it; but, in truth, teaches the diametric opposite:

> Drink today, and drown all sorrow;
> You shall perhaps not do it tomorrow;
> Best while you have it, use your breath;
> There is no drinking after death.

*Koheleth* does not teach an empty hedonism.

Nor is the lesson of *Koheleth* an embrace of the austerities and self-mortification that the Buddha had experienced in his seven years with the ascetics, or the self-punishing Mahavira, founder of the Jain tradition. What this book does teach, is to live our lives free from the aspiration to permanence, engaged with the things that make up our life but free from attachment to them.

Finding the Buddhist strand of *Koheleth,* we move beyond the frequently voiced dismissal of the book as preaching a destructive ethic. Nor is it, as some have mistakenly suggested, an endorsement of suicide. Those two perspectives accept the conventional wisdom about the nature of human life, but evaluate it negatively. Such nihilism or the advocacy of suicide requires us to understand life in conventional terms on the most superficial level, assuming the reality of "my" existence and the attendant primacy of "me" and "mine" in a concrete way that is not consistent with the idea of *havel.* The vision of *Koheleth* stands on a complete rejection of the conventional wisdom to which we are accustomed. *Koheleth* is not embracing destructive behavior. That would accept the reflex to be egocentric and selfish. *Koheleth's* lesson, most simply put, is that we should be *in* life, not *of* it. Do what we do, *Koheleth* teaches us, but do it free from attachment.

Scholars have told us that the message of *Koheleth* is not of a piece with normative biblical thought. They suggest that its meaning is most akin to the teaching of other cultures. I am in agreement with both these propositions. They have resolved its riddle by calling its message Stoic, or Epicurean. I believe it is most helpful to call it Buddhist. Reading *Koheleth* in the light of the teaching of the Buddha offers us the chance to see it in a new way. From this perspective, we can see *Koheleth,* not as a random collection of disjointed aphorisms, but as a book with a consistent, coherent message. Read in this light, *Koheleth* can talk to us in constructive ways, teaching us a lesson that can help us live our lives with less pain; and maybe even with equanimity, balance, and a sense of tranquility. How unfortunate that so many Jews have no idea that our Tanakh offers them access to such a precious resource.

# chapter 5

# Jains, Jews,
# and Under-the-Radar Values

What is the connection between the street sweepers in cities in India and one of the most influential thinkers of the twentieth century? When travelers visit India, they often report being puzzled by the sight of white-clad people wearing what look like surgical masks purposefully sweeping the ground in front of them. Our travelers might imagine that this is some kind of public works program of keeping the streets and sidewalks clean. Actually, it is a profound religious expression.

And the influential thinker? Here in America, we celebrate the strides in racial justice that were brought about through the heroic efforts of African American leaders like Martin Luther King, Jr. It is King who is responsible for channeling the energies of civil rights protesters toward non-violent resistance. King tells us that he learned non-violence from the work of the man widely credited with winning India's independence from England, Mohandas Gandhi. Gandhi called his philosophy *ahimsa*. Because Gandhi was Hindu, people assumed that the idea was part of his own religious background. But the fact is, that, though he was, indeed, Hindu, Gandhi was more spiritually eclectic than that. During his studies in England, he developed a great appreciation for elements of the Christian tradition. And back home in India, he absorbed the concept of *ahimsa* from a small minority religious community called the Jains.

And what is Gandhi's connection to those people whom our travelers imagined to be street sweepers? They are not employees of the sanitation department at all. They are Jains joined to Gandhi by their shared commitment to *ahimsa*. Their behavior, unfamiliar to our tourists, and perhaps strange to their eyes, is actually the way that they live out their commitment to *ahimsa* in their daily lives. Gandhi spoke of *ahimsa* as non-violence and made it the centerpiece of his political struggle. King learned of non-violence through Gandhi and applied it to his own work. For the Jains, *ahimsa* is something even more compelling than non-violence. It is the positive commitment to doing no harm. In action, it is better understood as reverence for life—for all life: for the lives of people of every group and every caste, and for all non-human life as well. As one Jain text instructs, "Do not injure, abuse, oppress, enslave, insult, torment, torture or kill any creature or living being." For Jains, *ahimsa* is the paramount value. It touches every aspect of their lives.

It is reverence for the life of creatures invisible to our sight that may live in water or fly through the air that causes Jains to wear masks. The fear that they might breathe in some tiny living being or ingest a microscopic living creature as they drink their water moves them to filter the air they breathe and the water they drink through the strip of cloth that looks to non-Jains like surgical masks. And it is *ahimsa* that causes them to sweep in front of themselves as they go about their lives so as not to inadvertently step on some small being. And it is this reverence for life that accounts for the simple, white clothing that they wear. Jains will not wear, or use in any way, cloth that involves harm to animals or people in its production. Reverence for lives of larger creatures makes them strict vegetarians and defines the sorts of professions in which they will not engage. Anything that causes harm to any living thing in any way, or benefits from the harm to animals, is forbidden to them.

In an environment where, as we have seen, different groups may be set against one another, reverence for the lives of their fellow human beings has made Jains tolerant of all people, regardless of whether they are Jains or not. It is what has caused Jains to reject the notion of the caste system, even while they believe in *samsara*, the wheel of reincarnation. *Ahimsa* requires tolerance and the active pursuit of decent relations between all people. It makes Jains opponents of any system that will disadvantage another human being. And it is what has made the Jains a pacifist tradition. Jains do not engage in wars, nor support warfare. And Jains will not engage in any activity or profession that promotes war or profits from it.

Remarkably, millennia before the environmental movement, Jains included concern for the welfare of the earth itself within the orbit of *ahimsa*. Jains, to this day, have a deep ecological awareness, and are active in efforts to protect the natural environment. Reverence for life is a far more life-defining creed than merely non-violence alone; and more encompassing than simply sweeping the ground before you as you walk. *Ahimsa* is a total, life-defining world view. It will have an unexpected resonance for Jews.

When Jews look at the Jains, they can't help but feel a certain affinity. Here is a religious group even smaller (two million people) than us. And it is one that has thrived over the millennia and remained resolutely faithful to its own traditions even as a minority within a much larger religious culture without compromising its unique identity. What Jews may not recognize is that embedded in their own tradition are values and practices that resonate with the Jains' *ahimsa*.

When Jews identify the values that are part of Jewish tradition, most will be quick to identify the Ten Commandments. Contemporary Jews will speak of *Tikkun Olam* in general terms of repairing the world and working for social justice. Some may be familiar with a somewhat broader spectrum of Jewish ideals. What many Jews may not know is that as a part of their tradition they inherit a constellation of values that resonate with *ahimsa*. Looking at the importance of *Ahimsa* to the Jains reminds us of the existence of some very specific traditional Jewish values which often seem to be unfamiliar to much of the Jewish community today. While nothing in Jewish tradition uses the phrase "reverence for life," that attitude is reflected in numbers of Jewish sacred texts. Let us look at a few of the themes in Jewish life that get thrown into sharper relief for us when we encounter *ahimsa*.

## Tzaar Baalei Chayim

Do Jews care about animals? Conventional wisdom has it that Jews (like Muslims) are terrified of and disgusted by dogs (dogs are seen as especially susceptible to madness). But, surprisingly, one recent survey of world-wide dog population found that, on a per-capita basis, the city that had the highest number of dogs was Tel Aviv. And if you have ever visited Jerusalem, you might have noticed the omnipresence of cats. So, clearly, the Jewish antipathy to animals is overstated. It is fair to say that the Jewish tradition is not going to be as thoroughgoing in its concern for animals as the Jains. It allows them to be employed for hard labor. It permits them to be eaten. And yet, Jewish tradition imposes limits on these actions that seem to represent moves in the direction of the values expressed in *ahimsa.*

If challenged to create a list of Jewish values, not many of us would think about including concern for the welfare of animals. But the fact is that in the repertoire of Jewish values there is a concept called *Tzaar Baalei Chayim:* attention to the suffering of living beings. In fact, this theme is already found in the Torah. To start with the most familiar, the Ten Commandments enjoin a weekly day of rest. The commandment, in testimony to the breadth of its concern for all people, is addressed to every category of person: masters and servants; males and females; homeborn and stranger. All are expected to desist from work. And then, in a way some may not have noticed, the commandment extends its scope of concern further:

> The seventh day is a sabbath to the Lord your God. In it you shall do no manner of work, you nor your son, nor your daughter, your male and female servants, nor your ox, nor your ass, nor any of your cattle....
>
> (Deuteronomy 5.14)

The same theme is restated elsewhere with even greater importance given to the rest of the animals involved, than the human beings:

> For six days you shall do your work, but on the seventh you shall rest, so that your ox and your ass shall have rest; and the son of your female servant and the stranger may be refreshed.
>
> (Exodus 23:12)

The Torah's extension of its sphere of concern is expressed in a number of concrete forms:

> If you see your fellow's ass or his ox fallen down along the way, you cannot hide yourself from him. You have to help him lift them up.
>
> (Deuteronomy 22:4)

> If you see [even!] your enemy's ox or his ass wandering around, you shall surely return them. If you see the ass of [even!] someone who hates you collapsed under its burden, you cannot just hold back from helping him. You must help him release [the animal].
>
> (Exodus 23:4–5)

All of these verses address two issues simultaneously. One strand talks about our responsibilities to our fellow human beings. In the Deuteronomy verse, you cannot take advantage of somebody's bad luck. If their animals have somehow escaped, not returning them is tantamount to theft. You owe it to them to return their property. In the verses from Exodus, the issue is one of how we treat our enemies, or people who hate us. Contrary to what Jesus is depicted in teaching in the Sermon on the Mount (Matthew 5:43), nothing in the Torah teaches us to hate our enemies. These Exodus verses are clear refutation of that. In a moment of distress, even our enemies are to be regarded as our fellow-human beings who deserve our concern and our help.

The second strand in all these verses is a visceral concern for the animals at the heart of the respective dramas. Lost or struggling, they, too, are objects of concern. Regardless of who the owner is, these unfortunate creatures require our care and attention. We cannot "hide ourselves" from giving them the assistance that they deserve. This is *Tzaar Baalei Chayim* in action.

Maybe you would argue that these verses really focused only on the inter-human dynamics and reflected no actual concern for the welfare of the animal participants in the dramas. Several injunctions from Deuteronomy should disabuse you of that. The first reflects concern for an ox, even to the disadvantage of its owner:

> You shall not muzzle an ox while it is working at grinding…[your] corn.
>
> (Deuteronomy 25:4)

Here the owner of the ox is using his animal to turn a millstone. The animal might, naturally, have its own interest in the food it was producing through its hard work. We can understand if the owner preferred to have all the milled grain for his own use. The Torah seems to understand the ox's interest in the project and takes the ox's side. Two other verses where we find some very specific, and touching, injunctions, are even more explicit in empathizing with the emotional sensitivities of animals:

You shall not plow with an ox and an ass together.
(Deuteronomy 22:10)

If you happen upon a bird's nest ... with a young bird or eggs with the mother sitting on them, you must not take the mother with the young. You absolutely must send the mother away if you are going to take the young.
(Deuteronomy 22:6–7)

These verses involve no benefit to any human being. All of them rest on empathy for the animals involved. The physical capacity of oxen and asses is different, not to mention their size. Being yoked together would cause distress, perhaps even physical pain to them. Concern for their feelings motivates this injunction. Similarly, an empathetic concern for the feelings of the mother bird is at the heart of the second prohibition. She is to be spared the emotional pain of having her young taken, and so she is sent away from the scene. The Torah, perhaps to our surprise, is concerned about the feelings of these animals, even if that causes inconvenience for human beings.

Perhaps the same sympathy for the maternal distress of an animal is at the basis of the familiar Torah injunction, "You shall not boil a calf in its mother's milk" (Exodus 23:19). The original intent of this commandment is lost to us. We have no idea what it might have meant to the first people who heard it. If we are familiar with the verse at all, it is because it became as the basis of one strand of Kashrut, the Jewish dietary rules. It became the basis of the practice of not eating milk and meat together, and of the often elaborate lengths to which many Jews go to keep dairy and meat in wholly separate realms. Some have suggested that the verse is about the prohibition of some form of fertility rite practiced by Israel's neighbors. Others have understood it on analogy to the Deuteronomy verses about the mother bird and her eggs, and have suggested that the intent is to spare the mother the pain of observing whatever it was that was being done to her young. Whether this interpretation of the verse is correct or not, the very fact that it is suggested at all reflects a sensitivity to *Tzaar Baalei Chayim*.

A final biblical thought on sensitivity to *Tzaar Baalei Chayim* is found in the Book of Proverbs.:

> The righteous person knows [is sensitive to] the life
>     [soul] of his beast.
> The "tender mercies" of the wicked are cruelty.
>
> (Proverbs 12:10)

Proverbs teaches that righteous people are attentive to the needs of their animals. The people who have no compassion for them are "wicked."

Later Jewish tradition, too, directed us to deal kindly and gently with animals, to be attentive to their needs. It was the rabbis (in Talmud Bava Metzia 32b) who created the very term *Tzaar Baalei Chayim* for the entire set of concerns which we have been addressing. The rabbis give us a Midrash/rabbinic narrative elaboration of the Torah which tells about the time Moses was, as it says in Exodus 3:1, "tending the flock of his father-in-law, Jethro." According to this narrative, one of the sheep in his charge ran off into the hills. Moses spent the whole day, and great effort, searching for the lost sheep, not stopping until he finally found it. It was while he was returning home carrying the exhausted and frightened sheep, the rabbinic story goes, that he encountered God at the burning bush. There God said to him, "Because you have been so tender to the lost sheep, I will send you to rescue My lost sheep, the people of Israel."

At the other end of the spectrum is the story of one of the rabbis who spoke cruelly to an animal on its way to slaughter:

"It was for this purpose that you were created!" As a result, it was decreed on high, that he should undergo great sufferings. Those sufferings ended only when, in the process of having his house cleaned, some small animals were found. When the rabbi ordered that they not be injured, another decree was issued on high: "Because he was compassionate, let us show compassion to him."

In one rabbinic teaching, the rabbis appear to condemn "Amorite" behaviors that they regard as cruelty to animals, such as slaughtering a rooster or chicken for their disruptive crowing, breaking eggs in front of chickens, and chastising ravens for their raucous cawing (Talmud Shabbat 67a).

The rabbis took for granted that "there is a requirement to prevent the suffering of animals" (Talmud Hullin 7b). The welfare and safety of animals is the subject of a conversation in Babylonian Talmud Shabbat 128b, where the rabbis sought to determine what actions are permitted in violation of the Sabbath. They agree that every effort must be made to save an animal that is in danger, even if it meant violating the Sabbath. Elsewhere in the Talmud (Brachot 40a), it is mandated that a person cannot eat their meal until their animals have been fed. The *Shulchan Aruch*/the Code of Jewish Law devotes chapters to the proper care for, and feeding of, one's animals.

The attitude toward the consumption of meat in Jewish law may appear paradoxical. It attempts to strike a balance between what is common human practice and concern for kindness to animals. On one hand Jewish law does allow for the eating—and slaughter—of meat. On the other, the laws of *kashrut* intentionally mitigate the pain to the animal in that process. Ritual butchers receive specialized training in slaughtering the animal while inflicting no pain on it. The laws of kosher slaughter are stringent in requiring that anything that would cause pain to the animal makes the meat unkosher.

But even this is not considered satisfactory by many Jews. A significant number, pointing to the value of *Tzaar Baalei Chayim*, say that a carnivorous diet, by its very nature, is inescapably cruel to animals. As a result, numbers of Jews advocate vegetarianism or veganism. There are numbers of Jewish vegetarian and vegan organizations. Many Jewish vegetarians and vegans assert that their approach is the highest form of kashrut, because it entails no suffering whatever.

## Concern for The World of Nature

Another Jewish value that calls for our concern to extend beyond the realm of interpersonal relations is known as *Ba'al Taschit*. Addressing our responsibility to the world of nature, it has its roots in a source that, in the context of the present subject, may appear incongruous. The unlikely basis for this value is a series of injunctions about the conduct of what we would call a just war:

> When you wage war against a city and besiege it for a long time in order to conquer it, you must not destroy its trees—wielding an axe against them. You may eat … [their fruit]; but you must not cut them down. Are trees of the field human beings that they could flee from you when under siege? Only trees which you know do not yield food may be… cut down.…

> (Deuteronomy 20:19–20)

On this single injunction, the rabbis constructed an entire edifice of opposition to wastefulness. The Talmud asserts that the general principle was the assumption that it is forbidden to "destroy anything of value" (Hullin 7b). Expanding on this idea, the rabbis call for avoiding excessive luxury in our diet and or clothing

(Kiddushin 32). They condemn the wasting of precious resources (Shabbat 67b), even the unnecessary tearing of clothes (Shabbat 105b). Rabbinic discussions demonstrate a sensitivity to the natural environment and an attentiveness to how we make use of it. The rabbis reflect a sense of the importance of the responsibility of caring for nature in the assertion that people can and should pray on behalf of a tree that ceases bearing fruit (Shabbat 67a). An early sort of ecological sensitivity found expression in the assertion, "Everything that the Holy One ... created in this world, He did not create anything for naught." (Shabbat 77b)

## Concern for Respectful Relations Among People

One of the harshest indictments of our Torah is that its system of rules is harsh, rigid, and ethnocentric. The Pharisees, as they are portrayed in the New Testament, are men of strict (and often hypocritical) application of "the Law." A familiar argument in the polemic battle of the early Christian community against its parent tradition was that, while Jewish "laws" were severe, inflexible, and xenophobic, the message of the new Christian faith was of kindness, compassion and love of all people. Polemics have the unfortunate quality of distorting the positions and character of the object of the attack. And this was no exception.

In fact, already, from the earliest stratum of rabbinic literature—and continuing on throughout Jewish history—the Jewish approach to its *mitzvot*/commandments contained a strand which maintained that whatever the "law" may require, it was to be ignored or overruled in response to overriding human realities. Central as the Sabbath was to Jewish practice, every stricture of its observance was to be violated for the purpose of saving a life—including, as we have seen, the lives of animals. Fasting on designated days, such as Yom Kippur, was a universal expectation. Except that some members of that "universe" were exempt, and, in fact, prohibited, from taking part in the fast: pregnant women, children, anyone who was sick, old, or infirm. Far from being rigid, the *mitzvah* system seems to have a built-in flexibility.

The Mishnah, the first layer of rabbinic literature, introduces a provision, with which many Jews are unacquainted, for addressing rules, which if applied rigidly, might cause interpersonal tension: *Mipnei Darchei Shalom.* The literal meaning of the phrase is "in the interest of promoting Shalom." We are accustomed to assuming that Shalom means the absence of war. And, of course, it does; but it includes wider shades of meaning beyond that. It is based on a three-letter root that conveys the sense of wholeness, intactness, completeness. It suggests a general wellbeing or tranquility. The term *Mipnei Darchei Shalom* is best understood in this broader sense. Throughout rabbinic literature, we encounter a collection of rulings that use the phrase *Mipnei Darchei Shalom* as a rationale for overturning or disregarding mandated practice in order to preserve the wholeness and completeness of the community: keeping it intact and harmonious. The underlying concern for harmony and the fundamental understanding that underlie *Mipnei Darchei Shalom* in themselves clearly have an affinity with the notion of *ahimsa.* But some of the specific applications of *Mipnei Darchei Shalom* show another, even more consequential, affinity.

Clearly, some of the practices and rules for which *Mipnei Darchei Shalom* are given as a rationale do serve the purpose of maintaining harmony within the community. *Mipnei Darchei Shalom* is given as the reason for intra-communal rules pertaining to such issues as: the order of reading (presumably during services from the Torah); setting traps for hunting and fishing; the filling of wells; the acquisition of property by presumably incompetent people (Mishna Gittin 5:8); the loan of kitchen wares (Gittin 5:9); and the exemption of priests from paying Temple dues (Shekalim 1:3). All of these are what we would call inward-facing concerns.

Yet others of the actions prescribed by the rabbis carry the significance of *Mipnei Darchei Shalom* beyond the boundaries of the community. As a result, we learn that non-Jews are to be accorded the same sympathetic concern as Jews. The same Mishnah verses that deal with intra-communal equity also include statements about non-Jews. Non-Jews cannot be prohibited from gathering gleanings of the field (Gittin 5:8). While Israelites are forbidden to work their fields during the Sabbatical year, no such restriction applies to non-Israelites, and an Israelite should feel free to greet them cordially as they are going about this work (Gittin 5:9).

The Gemara—the next level of the Talmud—commenting on, and building upon, the Mishnah, carries this mutuality with non-Jews even further. It requires that Jews must do the same things for non-Jews that they do for one another in the case of life-challenging moments. Jews must offer support to non-Jews in financial distress just as they would for fellow Jews; visit them when they are sick; and bury their dead (Gittin 61a). All these actions are described as being required *Mipnei Darchei Shalom*. The sense of the community whose Shalom is being promoted has been expanded to include Jews and non-Jews in a single harmonious whole. The recognition of the fundamental shared humanity of Jews and their neighbors, beyond the pursuit of intra-group tranquility, harmonizes very well with the teaching of tolerance and respect that makes up one element of the *ahimsa* taught in Jain tradition.

The rabbis believe that it is Torah that is the object of praise in Proverbs 3:17: "Her ways are ways of pleasantness and all her paths are Shalom"—understanding Shalom in its widest sense. One rabbinic teaching carries the idea even farther: "the whole Torah exists only for the sake of Shalom." With Shalom in its widest meaning as central to Jewish life, and the sense that Shalom demands both tranquility within a community and harmonious relations with those outside it, Jains encountering Jewish tradition could find a people imbued with values that they might well recognize as *ahimsa*.

## Commitment to Reverence for Life

How would you even translate the phrase *Reverence for Life* into Hebrew? In truth, Jewish religious texts do not make use of the term, or even an equivalent of it. And yet Jewish tradition offers many examples of instruction that reflect an underlying commitment to the ideal represented by this phrase, or make moves in its direction. We have already encountered the teaching that requires that every rule about the observance of Shabbat, so central to Jewish life, may be violated for the sake of saving a life. This must be regarded as a clear expression of what we would call reverence for life. There are other teachings which make moves in that direction, though not as explicitly.

As with *Tzaar Baalei Chayim,* it is clear that the biblical and later Jewish attitude toward reverence for life was not as thoroughgoing as in Jain practice. But, as with *Tzaar Baalei Chayim,* an examination of Jewish tradition can show us instances in which it makes moves in the direction of what we would identify as reverence for life. Indeed, we can find occasions when it seems to have moved away from the requirements of earlier teaching in the direction of that ideal. This was the case in the two consequential issues of capital punishment and the waging of war.

The case of the waging of war is, obviously, a complicated one in this context. Much as modern readers might prefer it to be otherwise, the Torah, unlike the Jain tradition, did not teach opposition to war. On the contrary, war and military victories are frequently described in an accepting, matter-of-fact way. In this, that ancient text is of a piece with the cultural context out of which it emerged. It reflects the values of a time and place in which the political environment seems to have been an embodiment of what the British philosopher Thomas Hobbes called the perpetual "war of all against all." Despite its frequent celebrations of the ideal of peace, nothing in the Torah condemns, or even criticizes, war. Indeed, it frequently seems to celebrate it, even to insist on the necessity of war in order for the Israelites to conquer the land of Canaan.

And yet. At the same time as it accepts the waging of war as a given, it makes a conceptual move to restrict it to some extent and to reduce its ferocity and destructiveness.

Several sections in chapter 20 of the Book of Deuteronomy have the effect of dramatically reducing the severity of the act of war-making itself by introducing changes in the way war was waged. In one innovation, any soldier who might wish to be excused from fighting, for any reason—including simple terror—must be granted an exemption (verses 1–9). This new approach to war seems to mean that any person who has personal objection to a particular war, or to war in general, cannot be forced to participate in it. As a result, their personal aversion to war is legitimized.

In addition, this same chapter contains the requirement, which we have already noted in another context, that when a city is being besieged, its fruit-bearing trees are not to be cut down: "Is the tree of the field a man, that it should be besieged by thee?" (verses 19–20). In this context, we can note that the destruction of trees constitutes an attack, not on a military target, but on the economic wellbeing of the civilian population. In such an act, a significant source of future livelihood is being destroyed. Here, Deuteronomy teaches that this assault on present and future civilian populations goes beyond what is acceptable in war.

In this same chapter, we read of even more dramatic modifications in the conduct of war. Israelite armies are required to offer besieged enemy cities the opportunity to sue for peace (verses 10–11). If a city surrenders peacefully, Israelite soldiers must in no way harm its residents. Even in cities which refuse to submit peacefully, non-combatants are not to be harmed. While Deuteronomy, like the rest of the Torah, does not express opposition to war, these various rules have the effect of confining its damage by limiting the scope of the battle and the classes of people subject to danger and harm.

The rabbis went even further in drawing limits on war. Mishnah Sotah, chapter 8, further restricts the pursuit of war by introducing the idea of two different categories of war. One type of war is regarded as defensive. Such wars are regarded as obligatory. There is no escaping the demand of self-defense. The other category is described as "discretionary." These are wars that a king might start for territorial expansion, the pursuit of spoils, or simply for self-aggrandizement. The rabbis ultimately create procedures and processes to restrict, even prevent, wars of this kind. Additionally, the rabbis are emphatic in reiterating the biblical concern for the protection of the lives of innocent civilians.

Jewish tradition does not totally reject warfare, as Jain tradition does. But it does progressively impose restrictions on the fighting of war. This has the effect of reducing it from being seen as a matter of course to, in appropriate instances, a necessary evil. Even in the case of permissible wars, there remain forms of battle that are regarded as unacceptable. In this way, Jewish tradition makes moves in the direction of diminishing the permissibility of war that echo the Jain rejection. We must assume that, like *Ahimsa*, this constriction of the acceptability of war must rest on what we call reverence for life.

We find a similar process at work in the case of capital punishment. The Torah accepts the prevailing cultural norm of the death sentence. At the same time, it introduces mitigations that impose some degree of limitation on its application. In this case, it limits the then-prevalent modes of its implementation in several ways. While neighboring cultures administered capital punishment for a wide variety of infractions, the Torah restricts the imposition of capital punishment to the crime of murder. In a cultural environment in which a retaliatory vendetta is allowed for the killing of a murderer's clansman in revenge for the murderer's crime, the Torah insists that the murderers alone are to be punished for their crime.

Further, the specific procedures involved in capital cases made the imposition of capital punishment more difficult. In a capital trial, a witness had to be so certain of their testimony that they would be willing to personally carry out the execution. Finally, the Torah insists on the distinction between premeditated murder and unintentional—accidental—killing. Only the premeditating murderer was to be punished. The person who was responsible for the accidental death of another is allowed to flee to one of six designated "cities of refuge" in which they may live without fear of vengeance from the family of the unfortunate victim of the accident that they had caused. These various restrictions, while not eliminating capital punishment (which we must understand as the taking—and devaluing—of life by organized society), have the effect of narrowing the range of people to whom it might be applied. As was the case in the issue of war, the rabbis were to carry this process even further.

To appreciate how the rabbis made moves in both these cases, we must start by recognizing the principle that seems to have been taken for granted among them: that the instructions of the Torah were inviolable and could not be overruled. But the decisions that these rabbis made often leave the impression that they also believed that Torah rules could be interpreted so narrowly that they would be virtually impossible to carry out in real life. And the result of the narrowing of the applicability of earlier rules could be in service of elevating the sanctity of life. The cases of the waging of war and of capital punishment are examples of clear biblical instruction which the rabbis interpreted so narrowly that they could not be put into practice—for no apparent reason other than that the idea that human life is valued so highly that it must take precedence over the instruction of the Torah itself.

The rabbis could not simply ban capital punishment, given that it was permitted in the Torah. But they could make its application so complicated and cumbersome that it became virtually impossible. To begin with, the court for a capital case had to consist of a panel of twenty-three, and in some cases seventy-one, judges, all of whom had to be of the highest character. Any judge who was considered to have a "cruel character" was automatically excluded from the panel. Complex procedures had to be carried out in precise fashion. Failure to follow those procedures would invalidate any imposition of capital punishment.

The very stringent requirements to serve as a witness in a capital case made it almost impossible for a defendant to be convicted. Witnesses, like the judges, had to be of impeccable character. No hearsay, second-hand testimony, or circumstantial evidence was allowed; only eyewitness accounts were admissible. As a result, witnesses had to have seen the entire crime as it was committed. But because witnesses were expected to be of high character, they could not be the sort of person who stood idly by and watched murder being committed. Instead, as any decent person would do, they had to have warned the perpetrator of the gravity of their actions and of the punishment they might be subjecting themselves to. But it remained conceivable that the perpetrator had not heard the admonition, and so for the witness to be considered credible, the perpetrator had to respond to the warning. Given all this, the likelihood of anyone's actually being sentenced to capital punishment was extremely low.

But in the unlikely case that such sentence was imposed, the complexities of the execution made it even more inconceivable. As a result of all these elaborate restrictions, one of the rabbis said that a court that oversaw an execution once in seven years should be considered a destructive tribunal. To which another of the rabbis said, "once in seventy years." Still two other rabbis, Rabbi Tarfon and Rabbi Akiba, said, "If we were members of the Sanhedrin, nobody would ever be put to death." The rabbis, concerned with the administration of justice though they were, were even more committed to the value—and the sanctity—of life. In this, they shared a close spiritual kinship with the Jains.

Spending time with the Jains, we come to admire the lesson of *Ahimsa*. We cannot help but appreciate it as the noble expression of a lofty ideal. If the whole world lived by it, the world would be a finer place. As Jews, the various aspects of *Ahimsa* cannot be wholly unfamiliar to us. Seeing Jewish tradition illuminated by the light of this encounter may throw into sharper relief an array of values in the teachings of our own people whose presence might not have stood out as clearly before. Sometimes seeing a lovely flower growing in a friend's yard helps us be grateful for its sister blossom blooming in our own.

# chapter 6

# Four Festivals, Two Traditions, One Common Threat

If you were to find yourself in India on the right days sometime in the month of October or November, during the Hindu month of Kartika, you would be likely to be caught up in one of the most joyous festivals of the Hindu calendar: Diwali. The dates are imprecise because the Hindu calendar, like the Jewish calendar, is a lunar calendar with a solar adjustment, which means that Hindu months are not precisely aligned with the Gregorian calendar. Much else is fluid in Diwali as well. Diwali actually is so beloved that its celebration is not limited to Hindus alone, but is also shared by members of the Sikh and Jain communities. And what is the holiday about? We will meet the same kind of fluidity that is so much a part of Hindu religiousness.

If you happened to be in the South of India, say in the city of Chennai, people would tell you that the holiday was a celebration of the destruction of the terrible demon Naraka after a furious battle at the hands of the god Vishnu, who incarnated himself as Krishna for the purpose. Good, they would tell you, has finally triumphed over evil. If you were in the north of India, in New Delhi or Jaipur, celebrants would inform you that the holiday is devoted to the climactic event of the Ramayana, one of the two great Indian epic narratives. They would regale you with the narrative of how Rama—understood to be another of the incarnations of Vishnu—assisted by his brother, Lakshmana, and the monkey god Hanuman, rescued his virtuous wife Sita from the clutches of the cruel and powerful demon king, Ravana (so fearsome that he had ten heads). And they would explain that Diwali commemorated the moment when the victorious Rama, and Sita, and their allies returned to their home in Ayodhya—which conveniently enough happens to be located in north India. And they would echo the familiar refrain that the holiday celebrates the triumph of good over evil, knowledge over ignorance, and light over darkness.

In Bengal, in the Eastern part of India, the holiday is identified with Kali puja, a day especially devoted to the worship of Kali, one of the consorts of the god Shiva. While in other parts of India she is depicted as hideous and terrifying, in Bengal she is seen as beautiful and benevolent. Her devotees tell stories of Kali's fierce battles with destructive demons of all kinds. As a result, she is seen, in herself, as the embodiment of the victory of good over evil.

Almost everywhere throughout India, the holiday is associated with the god Lakshmi. There are those who think of the holiday as commemorating her birthday, others who treat it as the anniversary of her marriage to Vishnu. But if there is one constant in almost all the different variants of Diwali, it is the veneration of Lakshmi, the god of prosperity and good fortune to whom people pray especially fervently for these benefits at this time.

Different as the various explanations of the holiday are, the way in which it is celebrated is the same almost everywhere. Well before the holiday itself begins, preparations for it have started. Homes are cleaned and decorated, inside and out. Everyone arranges their finest clothes. The celebration begins on the darkest night of the year and lasts for five days, into the time when light begins to increase. It is celebrated by the wearing of those fine clothes, the giving of gifts, elaborate meals for the extended family, and fireworks displays. But, far and away, the most prominent element of the holiday are the *diyas,* the small clay oil lamps, with which people decorate the insides of their homes, which they display in their windows, arrange on the outsides of their houses, and use to line public spaces. Lamps are everywhere. In fact, the word diwali, itself, is derived from the Sanskrit word meaning "row of lights."

Meanwhile, around the same time of the year, in other parts of the world, Jews are observing the holiday of Chanukah. For the eight nights of this festival, they remember the story of the Maccabees and their victory over the powerful army of the Syrian-Greek King Antiochus. They tell of the cleansing and rededication of the Temple in Jerusalem and of a great miracle that happened after the Temple was reclaimed and cleaned: the cruse of oil which contained only enough oil to maintain the flame of the Temple's eternal light for one day, yet somehow kept burning for eight. In honor of that cruse of oil, Jews will eat oil-based foods like *latkes,* fried potato pancakes, or *sufganiot,* jelly donuts. They will exchange gifts and play with the dreidel, the four-sided top emblazoned with letters on each side representing the phrase "a great miracle happened there." And, most importantly, on each night of the holiday they will light their Chanukah menorahs, nine-branched candelabrum: first one candle plus a helper candle on the first night, and then an additional candle each night until, by the last night of the holiday, all eight candles will be burning.

In terms of their manifest content, their stories, and the theological lessons drawn from them, the two holidays could not be further apart. But if we look at the ways in which the two festivals are celebrated, it is easy to identify the point at which the two holidays overlap. It is there, at that point of commonality, that we can find the common human core of both. And as we do that, we can, perhaps, appreciate a dimension of Chanukah that Jewish tradition does not deal with explicitly; yet one which may explain part of the real power of our celebration's hold on us.

It is no accident that both Diwali and Chanukah fall around the darkest time of the year—as does the Christmas of Western Christian tradition, the pagan Saturnalia, Dong Zhi of China, and Shab-e Yalda of Iran. And it is no coincidence that Chanukah and all the variants of Diwali celebrate some kind of victory.

Human beings do not like the dark. Perhaps it was a time of danger for our distant earliest ancestors: the time when vicious beasts or enemy assailants could sneak up on them. Darkness implied dread. And the increase of darkness must have filled them with anxiety about their increased vulnerability. The retreat of light also meant that the growing cold assailed their bodies, inflicting discomfort at best, and probably pain. Certainly, even for us, who are relatively insulated from the impact of nature, the reality of seasonal affective disorder testifies to the effect that the deprivation of light has on us. Somehow, the dark fills us with apprehension. We associate it with unpleasant, even bad, things. Light, on the other hand, has positive, pleasant, hopeful associations for us.

And from another perspective, the apprehension we feel about the descent into winter may be the residue of a very concrete and real ancient dread of the human species. In earlier times, winter was realistically a time of fear. The autumn harvest has been completed. No more food would grow for months, as the earth herself slept. The provisions from the fall harvest had to have been prepared and stored away. For the next three months, people's survival would hang in the balance. If enough food had not been laid up, people would not survive. It is easy to imagine that these distant ancestors of ours felt that, as the days grew darker, they were entering deeper and deeper into the realm of real jeopardy.

And, so, at the darkest time, Jews and Hindus (and Diwali-celebrating Sikhs and Jains) fill their surroundings with an abundance of light. In Chanukah, we actually act out the increase in light. As we light progressively more candles, we symbolically act out the bringing of light into the world. Hindus spread light throughout their homes and environment. Members of both communities celebrate light. And there is another important commonality. The stories told by both holidays exult in telling of a great victory. Demons are destroyed by one god or other. The oppressive might of Antiochus is crushed by the valiant Maccabees. Jews and Hindus alike rejoice in the triumph of good over evil. Both traditions speak in the same idiom. Both make explicit the inner meaning of their celebration. We can see that victory of good over evil as symbolic of the hoped-for victory of light over darkness. Diwali and Chanukah both reflect a certain common human anxiety about the encroaching dark. Both holidays vibrate with the hope that the dark will be defeated, and that light will prevail. Each in its own way is an attempt to contribute to that victory. The two holidays even share the byword that expresses the blend of the inner and outer meanings of the two celebrations: good triumphs over evil ... light over darkness.

For Jews, it is easy to remain focused on the externals of our holiday. It celebrates our history. It talks about religious freedom, and maybe about Jewish heroism in the face of foreign hostility. Even as we celebrate it throughout our lives, we might not recognize the inner, shared, human resonance of the holiday. Seeing it in "conversation" with a holiday from a very different tradition brings that inner meaning to the surface for us. Our celebration of Chanukah can be even more meaningful because of that.

Six weeks after Diwali and Chanukah, during the Gregorian calendar's February and March, both communities find themselves celebrating again. For each, these later festivals have a very different character from the earlier ones. Chanukah and Diwali, while joyous, are relatively serious. Neither is somber. But both are carried on in an orderly way with a kind of propriety. Both are happy but staid. After all, they tell serious stories grown in response to serious life situations. The later holidays feel very different. They seem almost what someone called, in a different context, "irrationally exuberant." And with good reason.

In India, in the last month of the lunar/solar calendar, Phalguna, on the day of the full moon, Hindus celebrate Holi. What is it all about? As with Diwali, the story about the meaning of the holiday will differ among different groups. Shaivites, devotees of the god Shiva, celebrate the holiday as a commemoration of the devotion of Shiva and his wife Parvati and the way she pulled him back from his absorption in ascetic practice to live in this world—with her—with the help of Kamadeva, the god of love. Vaishnavites, worshippers of the god Vishnu, tell a more elaborate story about one devotee of Vishnu, Prahlada, whose life was imperiled by his demon aunt Holika. For them, Holi celebrates how Vishnu, in his incarnation as Narasimha, the man-lion, rescued his devotee and incinerated Holika in a great fire. For those who worship Krishna, another incarnation of Vishnu, the holiday tells the story of how Krishna and his consort Radha expressed their love for each other by applying color to one another's face.

We shall see how elements of these various stories play a role in the way the holiday is celebrated. As is always the case, we can speculate whether the various elements from the stories were given tangible expression in the particular practices, or whether the various stories emerged at some time after the practices to explain their origins. In the end, of course, that kind of question is of much more interest to students of religion than to the people who celebrate the holiday. What is of real importance to us, here, is that, once again, as was the case with Diwali, however much the backgrounds of the various stories may differ, the fundamental aspects of the way in which the holiday is celebrated, with a little variation, are consistent. However differently from your neighbor you may tell the story of Holi, you both celebrate it in the same way.

The holiday is generally spoken of as a celebration of love, a theme captured in the stories of Shiva and Parvati and Krishna and Radha. Virtually every celebration will begin the night before the day itself with a large communal bonfire, as included in the story of Vishnu as Narasimha. It will end with people putting on finery and—despite having discarded their conventional roles during the day—return to their customary identities by evening. They will spend that second evening going around, visiting and feasting with family and friends. It is what happens during the day between the two evenings that is the real heart of Holi.

Fueled by the generalized use of intoxicants, the day itself is one of wild abandon and extravagantly outlandish, even transgressive, behavior. People douse one another with water and shower each other with brightly colored powder (reminiscent of the story of Krishna and Radha). The day is characterized by the din of all manner of loud noises: the blowing of horns and the beating of drums. A kind of anarchy prevails. Decorum and respectability are cast aside. On this day, pleasure and joy take precedence. The byword of Holi is *"Bura na mano, Holi hai*—Don't take offense, it's Holi."

More shockingly, Holi is characterized by the overturning of conventional social norms and even cultural and religious taboos. This is exemplified by the frenzied way that the water and colored powder are thrown around in which, by the very nature of the actions, people behave with overt rudeness to one another. While normally people would be proscribed from speaking in vulgar or obscene ways, on Holi such behavior is encouraged.

A significant feature of Holi is the dissolution of social boundaries, ordinarily so strictly maintained and so important in India—a society which distinctly separates people by their various identities. On Holi, those barriers go down and everyone celebrates together: men and women, old and young, rich and poor, employee and employer. The identity roles which define people and separate them so strictly during the rest of the year dissolve during Holi (as if by the water thrown around with such abandon). The patterns of authority which traditionally define society are, for this one day, annulled. Actions which would be considered scandalous during the rest of the year are allowed, even expected, on Holi: children are disrespectful of their elders, students mock their teachers, women talk back to their husbands in public and even insult them. What we see in Holi is the wholesale overturning of the very rules which hold the society together during the rest of the year, the nullification of the patterns that govern the most charged social interactions.

The most transgressive of these has been saved for last. Holi involves a shocking behavior which subverts the very basis of Indian society. While for the rest of the year caste propriety is the most significant social norm of Hindu society, on Holi it is aggressively violated. Normally, members of lower castes are excluded from public celebrations. On Holi they are included. Even more radically, Brahmins and members of other upper castes, in explicit violation of rules of decorum held rigidly during the rest of the year, are, on this day, expected to touch and allow themselves to be touched by members of lower castes. In short, what we see is a day set apart from the rest of the year in its loosening of conventional propriety and overturning of social norms.

At this same time, Jews are observing the holiday of Purim. Today many Jews celebrate Purim only by reading the Megillah, the biblical book of Esther, sounding the *gragger* (noise-maker), eating Hamantaschen, and maybe wearing a costume or mask. In the past, Jews celebrated Purim in a more intense way that was more expressive of its inner reality. Let us take note here of a custom, still widely practiced, that seems shoehorned into the more raucous aspects of Purim that we will shortly be observing. It was traditionally Purim, not Chanukah, which included the giving of gifts. One common feature of the day was *shalach manot*, the sending of dainties and treats to friends and families.

Purim is radically different from all other Jewish celebrations. If she were a person, you would characterize her as raucous, rowdy, and unruly. Irreverent and disrespectful. If she were your daughter, you would lose sleep at night. The other holidays, holy days, and festivals on the Jewish calendar have a fundamental decorum. They may be joyous and happy, but they are orderly. Even when they celebrate great deliverances, the liturgies of those celebrations can be solemn (think of the Passover Seder). The other holidays commemorate significant historical moments or offer the opportunity for serious spiritual engagement. Purim is not about any of these. Instead, it is, as it has been traditionally celebrated, a day wholly given over to encouraging behaviors that are forbidden during the rest of the year.

Jews are, according to conventional wisdom, a relatively abstemious people. On Purim they are encouraged to drink in excess—until they "cannot distinguish between the pious Mordechai and the wicked Haman." Gambling is prohibited during the rest of the year. On Purim, that prohibition is lifted and what is normally forbidden is given communal sanction. Of greater significance, all the norms and conventions that normally organize society are turned on their heads. Elders, teachers, and parents, who usually receive respect, on this day are ridiculed and mocked. Wives insult and demean their husbands in public. Men wear women's clothes and vice versa. In their outlandish costumes and masks, it is impossible to tell the difference between rich and poor, philanthropist and beggar, teacher and student. In short, on Purim the normal order of the community virtually disappears.

And the disorder extends even into the sacred precincts of prayer and study. The very forms of religious observance become the object of derision. Teachers set aside their normal curriculum and offer "Purim Torah," ridiculous, distorted, sometimes vulgar, versions of the serious lessons they would normally offer. The primary literary mode of Purim is not piety, but parody. When the Torah is the sacred text read during services, it is accorded solemn and serious devotion (a subject to which we shall return in the next chapter). On Purim, in itself a sort of parody of the normal reading of scripture, the text before the congregation is the Megillah, the Book of Esther (itself a very strange book to be included in a religious scripture): a book of foolishness, in which people behave in buffoonish ways, events turn out to be the diametric opposite of what would normally be expected, the breaking of norms is celebrated, and things are consistently turned on their heads. Hardly treated with the seriousness of sacred text, its reading is accompanied by the cacophony of graggers, the stamping of feet, and enthusiastic eruptions of denunciation of the name of the villainous Haman—all of which make the text virtually impossible to hear over the din. The byword of Purim is "On Purim, all things are permissible." What are we to make of this disruption of social propriety and religious decorum?

When we look at Holi and Purim, the manifest content—the stories told about them, and their theological purpose—are clearly different. Radha and Krishna, Parvati and Shiva, and Vishnu, do not exist in the same universe as Esther and Mordechai. Haman, dark and treacherous as he is, is no Holika. The salvation of the Jews is far removed from Parvati pulling Shiva back from ascetic absorption. But if we look at the ways in which the two holidays are observed, the forms in which they are celebrated, and the social implications of these forms, we cannot escape seeing how very similar they are. These festivals, emerging from different religious traditions, with very different theological messages, turn out to be structurally identical.

Holi and Purim—and other holidays taking place at precisely the same time: Mardi Gras in New Orleans, Carnival in Rio de Janeiro, and the countless other carnivals around the globe—share the same structural elements. They include a raucous atmosphere; excessive consumption of intoxicants; masks and costumes; the din of tumultuous noise; and the transgression of social norms—even, perhaps especially, the most important ones—outlandish behavior; the reversal of traditional roles; interpersonal rudeness; mocking respected institutions and people of authority. Structurally, these holidays are the same. Why is this so?

This structural affinity grows out of a deeper human connection. The two holidays—and those other celebrations as well—share a commonality of function. They both represent a response to a common human reality. It is in that deeper commonality that we can discover aspects of Purim that can add, perhaps unanticipated, layers to our appreciation of it.

There is a shared functional role in the historical origins of these holidays. They don't fall on the calendar where they do by accident. Both come at the very onset of spring as winter begins to retreat. Winter was, for the earliest ancestors of all humanity, a time of scarcity, darkness, and real fear. The onset of the change of seasons meant that our ancestors would no longer be confined to their cold, dark, cramped quarters. They could begin to go outside again, to mingle with a wider swath of people. It would make sense that the emotional response to this return to the world of nature would be exuberance.

And, as we've noted, the uncertainty that was associated with winter had real cause. Food did not grow during the winter. Our forebears had to store produce from the fall harvest and were forced to allocate it sparingly in the hope that it would last until the next season's harvest. All winter they lived with the anxiety that, if they had not stored enough provisions, or if something were to happen to the provisions they had laid up, the consequences would be tragic. Thus, the arrival of spring truly represented a time of new beginnings. This was the time of new planting and harvesting; new food and new hope. It is natural that the arrival of such a time would be one of relief and rejoicing.

Emotionally, the arrival of spring marked the end of the time of the anxiety about scarcity. Our human forebears had suffered through self-imposed deprivation all winter and had endured the constraints of rationing their stored-up provisions. It was against this background of the end of scarcity and the promise of new abundance that people felt liberated from the fear of insufficiency. Now they were free to eat without anxiety … or restraint. With the arrival of the new growing season, they felt they could afford to treat themselves lavishly, even extravagantly. In such a frame of mind, ostentatious displays of consumption do not seem inappropriate. They could feast, as at the end of Holi, or afford to send gifts of food, as with *shalach manot*. It is perhaps not accidental that the story of Esther begins with one feast and that its climax—the final foiling of Haman—occurs at another.

The removal of a source of fear inspires a profound sense of release in any of us. These survivors of winter's peril could reasonably be expected to be intoxicated with relief and hope. It was only natural for them to join together in a shared communal indulgence in that exhilaration.

These festivals take place at the start of the planting season. We can assume that, in their most distant agricultural origins, there were elements of fertility rites, expressions of hope that the earth would yield a rich harvest, and effort to assure it. Fertility rites have conventionally included such elements as dance, chants, frenzy, and intoxication. In many cultures, such fertility rites have also incorporated a sexual component. Human coupling became an act of sympathetic magic inducing the hoped-for fecundity of the earth. In Holi, we see a residue of this in the holiday's designation as a celebration of love, of the presence of Kamadeva, the god of love, and of the theme of love and attraction in the stories of Radha and Krishna, and of Parvati and Shiva. In Purim, such sexuality is implicit in the story of Esther that is the basis of the holiday: the insistence of King Ahashuerus that his then-wife Vashti dance (naked—in the way the rabbis elaborate the story) for his assembled friends; the "contest" in which he selects a new queen from all the young women of his country; the preparation and selection of Esther for that role; and most significantly, Esther's bed, on which the most transparently sexual, climactic events of the book occur: Esther's retiring to her bed where, at least in the eyes of the king, Haman attempts to ravish her. In the celebration of the holiday, this sexuality presents itself in sublimated form in the general frenzy of the celebration and in the overt behaviors such as cross-dressing and the inversion of gender roles which are permitted, indeed encouraged, on this day alone.

Another thing these celebrations share is their intensely public nature. They are acted out in group settings and shared public spaces. Neither of them has the introspective, personal quality that characterize other holidays in each tradition. They take place in the public square, as opposed to the more serious home observance of each of the traditions, like daily puja of the Hindu home, or the family Seder which will take place for Jews one month later. Sociologists see public festivals like this as building an enhanced sense of group unity, promoting social cohesion.

Paradoxically, these holidays, contrary to what we might expect, serve to enforce the norms of the community. Suspending those norms for a day serves as a testimony to just how important they are under normal circumstances. The temporary suspension of normative behavior may also serve as a pressure release. Members of the group who may chafe at conventional norms are allowed to express their resentment, give it vent in the most public—and collectively celebrated—way possible, and then return to the normal order of things. After the conclusion of that temporary suspension, people can return from the transgressive moment reaffirming their community's fundamental structure, re-embracing its norms and committing themselves to them anew. Paradoxically, by temporarily discounting its norms and then returning to them, the community reaffirms their adherence to them.

Seen in the context of Holi, we can recognize new dimensions in Purim: the role it has played—and continues to play, even without being recognized, in Jewish life. We get a sense of its roots in an agricultural festival, celebrating the arrival of spring and retaining elements of a fertility rite. We recognize it as involving some of the frenzy, excess, and riotous behavior that characterizes Holi (and other carnival celebrations). Like Holi (and most of the other holidays in the Jewish calendar) we can see it as very much connected to the season in which it occurs. And, as with Holi, we can appreciate its role in serving to bond the community, strengthen social cohesion, and reinforce group norms. Seen in this light, Purim becomes a more important and consequential holiday than the "minor festival" role to which we usually relegate it.

When we look at all four of the holidays we have explored in this chapter, we can appreciate all of them as expressions of human responses to common human realities. Specifically, with these four holidays, we notice that in both traditions they function as bookends to the deprivations of winter. Chanukah and Diwali give voice to the apprehension that flows from the shrinking domain of light; Purim and Holi rejoice in the imminent arrival of the season of light and warmth and abundance. Looking at these holidays, which are usually considered in isolation, collectively and across the boundaries of tradition, we develop a new appreciation of the human realities out of which all of them arise.

# chapter 7

# It is a Tree of Life

It is midnight at the *Harmandir Sahib*, the Golden Temple, in Amritsar, in the Punjab region of northwest of India. A selected group of Sikh dignitaries are preparing a sanctuary, as they do every night at this time, cleaning it diligently, purifying it with milk and water to prepare for the arrival of the Guru, the worldwide leader of the Sikh community. (Usually in India, the term *guru* simply means teacher. For Sikhs it is the title of their supreme leader—beginning with the first leader, Guru Nanak). In three hours, as they do every early morning, the leaders of that community will make their way to the chamber of their Guru to rouse the leader and escort them to the newly purified sanctuary. With whisks waving above the Guru to purify the air, they transfer their Guru from bed to a waiting palanquin (like an elaborately decorated hand-carried chariot). Amidst great celebration, the sounds of chanting, blowing horns, and beating drums, the Guru is borne to the sanctuary where an even greater crowd is waiting in rapt anticipation. At the entrance of the sanctuary, the leader of the band of dignitaries lifts the Guru from the palanquin and, placing the Guru on his head....

Wait. Do you think you have read this wrong? Perhaps I have confused you. Maybe you thought that the Guru was a revered personality, like the Pope, or the Chief Rabbi of some locality. But for the Sikhs, the worldwide leader of their community is not a person at all. The guru being borne to the sanctuary is the Guru Granth Sahib, an immense volume of the Sikhs' sacred text. Every morning in Amritsar, the ceremony is repeated. The Guru Granth Sahib is borne ceremoniously to the sanctuary. Then it is placed on the reading stand, the wrappings that have protected it are undone, and the beautifully decorated cloth with which it has been covered on this journey is carefully removed. Finally, one of the leaders of the community reads from it aloud to the assembled crowd—and, via broadcast, to Sikhs around the world. For the remainder of the day, the book will be placed in a display case and people will reverently file by, moved to be in its very presence.

A similar scene is reenacted everywhere Sikhs gather for worship. In every gurdwara, the Sikh house of assembly, the world over, the Guru Granth Sahib will be taken out of its special place of repose and borne with great pomp and ceremony to the assembled group of faithful waiting with great expectation. With whisks purifying the air above it, it is carried into the room on the head of the leader of that local community. The gathered faithful chant and sing, their eyes fixed on the sacred book, until it is placed on a reading stand. Then with great solemnity, the wrapping is unwound, and the beautiful covering is removed. Finally, the leader proceeds to intone the words of the sacred text. At the conclusion of the reading, the Guru Granth Sahib will be carefully wrapped, covered, and returned to its special resting place.

How did it happen that the fifth largest religious group on the planet came to be led, not by a human Sikh, but by a book? The book itself was assembled over many generations, starting with Guru Nanak, the first Guru, and including the writing of other Sikhs, and—unusual in sacred scriptures—non-Sikhs as well. Throughout Sikh history, the book had been revered. But in 1708, its role changed dramatically. You may remember Guru Gobind Singh, the tenth Guru. At the time we met him, we identified him as "the last Guru." That was not precisely correct. What we should have said is that he was the last *human* Guru. The final instruction that he gave before his death was that, following him, leadership of the community would no longer to be passed to a human being. From his death on, Sikhs would be led by, and take their instruction directly from, their sacred text. Thus it was that, for the last four centuries, the most revered and important role in Sikh life has been held by a book. Why should this be of any interest to Jews?

A familiar axiom has it that "God, Israel, and Torah are one." It is easy to say (actually, there is a song that has put these words to music, so it is even easy to sing). But it is not so easy to understand. What does the axiom mean? Max Kadushin, a 20th-century scholar, unwraps this idea in his theory of "organic Judaism." He suggests that it is impossible to talk about anything authentically Jewish without involving all the members of this triad. In fact, he teaches, you cannot Jewishly talk about any one of them without reference to the other two. Another scholar, Jacob Neusner, has described Jewish religious tradition as "The Way of Torah."

So Torah becomes an inseparable part of Jewish life. And yet, for Jews, Torah is so omnipresent that it becomes easy to lose sight of it altogether. Every time we go to synagogue we see it. So why should we talk about it as so special? Let's talk about what Torah means. We are told that *Torah* is a word that means teaching. And it does. But it carries levels of meaning beyond and beneath that.

Actually, Torah has layers of meaning. Think of the term as a series of concentric circles. It means, of course, the Chumash, the Five Books of Moses as it is read in Hebrew. The next circle would be that same text read in any language. Torah studied in English, or French, or Amharic (the language of the Jews from Ethiopia) is still Torah. The rabbis called those previous levels "the written Torah," the Torah that is written down, the Torah that Jewish tradition regards as being given to Moses at Sinai. The rabbis introduced a level of Torah beyond that, the next concentric circle. They called it the Oral Torah. The spoke of it as being given at Sinai as well, but passed on orally from generation to generation, until it reached them and they gave it voice. The Oral Torah finally got written down, most prominently in the Talmud, with its two layers: Mishnah and Gemara. That is Torah, too. And so is this book. The next, and outer layer of our concentric circles, is any teaching about Jewish life. What in English is called a sermon is, Jewishly, referred to as a *d'var Torah*, literally a word of Torah. Learned Jews will often greet one another by inquiring "give me a *vort Torah*"—another way to say a word of Torah. The correct response to such a request is not to say something like, "In the beginning God created the heavens and the earth." Rather it is to share some new insight about the text. Studying Torah, teaching Torah, is called doing Torah. Reading this book, you are doing Torah too.

If you have envisioned these concentric circles in your mind, or have been compulsive enough actually to draw them, you will probably have noticed that I have perpetrated a trick on you. I skipped the innermost circle. Because that is what I really want us to look at. That innermost Torah, the physical scroll, is the one people are so familiar with that they hardly recognize the exceptional role it plays in Jewish religious life. That innermost circle, called the Sefer Torah, is a parchment scroll containing the Hebrew text of the Five Books of Moses. And, just as it is at the center of our concentric circles, it is at the center of Jewish life. And yet Jews hardly think of their relationship to this scroll as extraordinary.

But having been to Amritsar, seeing the Sefer Torah in the light of the Guru Granth Sahib, perhaps we can appreciate it as the remarkable religious phenomenon that it is. I want us to pay attention to the Sefer Torah, the Torah scroll itself—that physical object that is the tangible, physical embodiment of everything that goes by the name Torah. The Guru Granth Sahib makes us aware of the sheer physicality of our most precious possession, the Torah.

The very creation of a Torah scroll is considered a holy act and it is not something done casually. If you wanted to send someone a letter—in the days before email—you would grab a piece of paper and a pen and just start writing. That is not how a Sefer Torah comes into the world. You have to be a specially trained scribe—a *sofer*—to create a Sefer Torah. And you have to devote your life to this holy calling. The very parchment on which the words are written must be specially prepared, as well as the ink and even the quill pen that you will write with. Even the handles of the two staves, around which the parchment is rolled, must be specially prepared. And they have a name. Each is called—in tribute to the profound importance of the text—an *etz chayim:* a tree of life. The name echoes the rabbis' understanding of the words from Proverbs 3:18. Whatever the words may have meant in Proverbs, for the rabbis, they were a tribute to Torah: "It is a tree of life to those who hold it fast and all who cleave to it find happiness."

To be a sofer, you have to prepare yourself spiritually before you can start your work, and again every time you return to your sacred task. Writing a Sefer Torah will take you six months to a year, depending on your level of proficiency. It is no small commitment. For the sofer, writing Sifrei Torah is his (and in more recent times, in the liberal streams of Jewish life, her) very life. And should the Sefer Torah become damaged or worn in later years, a congregation will have a sense of urgency to fix it as quickly as possible. The congregation will not have just anyone take care of the problem. A damaged Sefer Torah must be maintained and repaired by a sofer.

When a congregation acquires a Sefer Torah they do not treat it casually. First, they will have a special service of welcome and a celebration. (And let us note, congregations regard being home to a Sefer Torah to be a source of pride. Wealthier congregations may own more than one—indeed, as many as their resources allow.) After the congregation welcomes their Sefer Torah, they will dress it regally. Among Ashkenazi Jews, whose roots are in Eastern Europe, the Sefer Torah will wear a *gartel,* a sash, around the rolled parchment to hold it securely, and a *k'tonet*—Torah cover—often a beautifully designed piece of art in itself. It will wear an *ephod,* a breastplate. In many congregations, the Torah literally wears a crown. In some congregations, instead of a crown the Sefer Torah wears *rimonim,* pomegranates, elaborate decorations made of precious metal on each upper *etz chayim* of the scroll. The Sefer Torah in even the humblest synagogue is dressed in exactly the same special garments the Book of Exodus describes the High Priest as wearing. Among Sephardic Jews, whose ancestry traces back to Spain, the Sefer Torah will be covered in an elaborate case of wood or metal, perhaps decorated with precious gems, that serves the same purpose of celebrating and enhancing the parchment text. Often even this encased Sefer Torah is covered with a decorated cloth.

Once the scroll is welcomed, the congregation will not simply place it in a storage room or closet. It will not even be kept it in its library. The Sefer Torah will be housed in a special cabinet in the sanctuary called the *aron kodesh*, holy ark. The name is taken from the chest in which Moses and the Israelites carried the Ten Commandments during the forty years of the Exodus. There are no rules dictating the design of Jewish sanctuaries, no formal pattern. Sanctuaries will vary widely in architectural design. But one thing we can predict about every sanctuary: it will have an ark. And in every synagogue, the design of the ark is not simply functional, but as elaborate and beautiful as the means of that congregation allow. Often it is very much a work of art in its own right, as befits its contents.

Significantly, in most congregations the ark is the visual focal point of the sanctuary or chapel. It is what your eye is drawn to as soon as you enter. In the house of worship of any religious tradition, the focal point is a visual cue about what is really of importance to that religious tradition. In Hindu temples, the focal point is the image of the god. In a Christian church, the focal point is often a crucifix. In a synagogue, the focal point is the ark, in recognition of the role of the Sefer Torah or Sefer Torahs that it holds.

The role of the Sefer Torah in worship reminds us of just how central it is to Jewish life. The Torah is read as part of the service every Shabbat and holiday as well as on Mondays and Thursdays during the week. When it is time for the Torah to be read, it is not just removed from the ark and carried directly to a reading stand.

The reading of the Torah makes up a special, elaborately choreographed, section of the service. This Torah service has a different emotional quality than other parts of the service. There is a special intensity to it. As the Sefer Torah is removed from the ark, people stand at their places and remain standing until the covering of the Sefer Torah has been removed and the scroll is placed on the reading stand.

In most congregations, between the removal of the scroll from the ark and the actual reading, while people are still standing, the Sefer Torah is carried in procession through the congregation (much as images of saints are carried through streets of cities in Catholic countries, or icons among Eastern Orthodox). The emotional atmosphere is more charged at this moment than at any other point in the service. As the Sefer Torah is carried through the congregation, it is conventional for people to reach out to touch the Sefer Torah, even kiss it. The Sefer Torah is then read, and afterward replaced in the ark, also with much ceremony.

This procession of the Sefer Torah through the congregation is even more intense on the holiday Simchat Torah, literally "rejoicing in the Torah." On this holiday, the last of the weekly Torah reading portions, the last chapter of the book of Deuteronomy, is read, immediately followed by the reading of the first portion, the first chapter of Genesis. Custom has it that we hold our breath after the reading of Deuteronomy and do not exhale until Genesis has been begun. The high point of this particular service comes before the actual reading from the scroll. When the Sefer Torah is (or all the scrolls, if a congregation has more than one, are) taken from the ark, there are numerous rounds of processions through the congregation accompanied by singing—and, often, dancing—and an almost carnival-like air of boisterous excitement. The reading of scripture, of course, is the focus, but before that takes place, one would not be amiss in assuming that the Sefer Torah itself was being celebrated.

The physical Sefer Torah, not simply the text it contains, seems to be an object of veneration. And it plays another role. At the points during a worship service when the most important prayers are being offered, the Ark is opened and the congregation rises to its feet. To the observer unfamiliar with Jewish worship, it may well appear as if the Torah scrolls were somehow serving as a kind of conduit for the words being offered; as if the Sefer Torah were treated as an intercessor, transmitting upwards the words of the worshipper—as do icons for Eastern Orthodox, and images of saints, and the saints they represent, for Catholic Christians—and the images before which Hindus do *puja*.

In the end, we would be incorrect in imagining that what we have seen suggests that the Sefer Torah, itself, is really an object of worship, or even that it is actually believed to play the role of intercessor. Nothing in Jewish tradition teaches that. Jews would be surprised to hear anyone even suggest that. And yet, having visited Amritsar and seen the role of the Guru Granth Sahib, it is fascinating to see the extent to which Jewish behavior patterns resemble those of the Sikhs. There can be no denying that Jews display a veneration for the scroll itself and conduct themselves as if it played some kind of intercessory role. Torah worship, or Torah as intercessor, plays no role in Jewish belief. But it is very much part of the form of Jewish practice.

What learning we can take from this? The veneration displayed toward the Sefer Torah reminds us just how central Torah is to the Jewish religious tradition. Torah—not in terms of the scroll, but in terms of those later rings of the concentric circles of Jewish learning—is at the heart of the life of the Jewish people. The Sefer Torah becomes the symbol, the emblem, of Torah in its largest sense. And it is on behalf of that larger meaning of Torah that it becomes the object of celebration and honor. It is in that larger sense that we can understand the teaching that joins together all the crucial elements of Jewish life: "God, Israel and Torah are one."

# Afterword

Well, there you have: it a whirlwind religious tourism visit to India. Together we have traversed thousands of miles and thousands of years with the goal of ... a deeper understanding of the Jewish tradition. Somewhat paradoxical, I know. I hope that my discussion of two traditions in tandem did not compromise my objectivity in describing them. I hope you did not feel that my description of the various Indian traditions was pejorative in any way (we all know that comparison can be invidious) or gave the impression that I was making value-laden judgments about them. Nothing could have been further from my intent. On the contrary: I hope my presentation of them was respectful and appreciative. I continue to be awed by the compelling quality, the beauty—and the deep sincerity of adherents—of those traditions.

And on the other hand, I hope you did not see the project of this book as syncretistic, trying to meld two separate things into one large new thing. There are people who believe that the purpose of inter-religious engagement is to find "the things we share." I am not one of them. As we meet people from different religious backgrounds, I believe in the importance of recognizing, acknowledging, even celebrating, our differences. There is beauty in them. I hope I have written a book that reflects the belief that our differences are to be honored. They are what give each of our traditions their own distinct character.

As I said when we began, I write as a student deeply fascinated by, and admiring of, the religious traditions of India ... and as a committed and engaged Jew. On our journey, I have sought to celebrate the genius of a people whose understanding of God grew over generations—and to throw into relief the complexities of that understanding as it arrived at its full expression. Looking at the Jewish understanding of God as we have, we can recognize just how remarkable and sublime it was and appreciate the full implications of the great contribution we have made to human understanding. We have been biblical archaeologists, uncovering layers of meaning in a book that might otherwise be indecipherable and remain closed and unread. We have explored some of our practices and uncovered depths that may be hidden to us by their very familiarity.

Above all, it is my sincere hope that you come away from reading this book with a deeper appreciation of your own Jewish tradition; that you can see in sharper relief aspects of it that you hadn't recognized before; that you come to see some of its elements more fully and appreciate depths in it that you had not plumbed before. I hope it opens doors of Jewish life for you and offers you the opportunity for new fulfillment and joy.

# Acknowledgments

Of writing many books there is no end.

Ecclesiastes 12:12

There is a certain paradox involved in the getting of this book—or any book—into the hands of you, its readers. A book begins with a particular idea seizing the author, in this case me, and driving him or her to spend untold hours isolated at their desk, a prisoner of the mania that compelled them to conceive of the work in the first place. This demands a certain degree of isolation from your loved ones as you are consumed with moving the words and ideas trapped in your head onto the printed page. Inevitably, for a period of time you are removed from the normal routines of family life and inaccessible to the people who are most important to you. Writing a book wreaks havoc on family life. So, I want to express my thanks to my wife Gail and our daughter Leah, who put up with prolonged and unpredictable absences while I retreated to my desk relentlessly until this book was completed. I am more grateful than I can express for their forbearance to me and their tolerance of my preoccupation while I was giving birth to this book.

And now the paradox. While the writing of a book is an intensely individual undertaking, its progress from manuscript to the text you hold in your hands is very much a collaborative effort. As a reader, I confess I have never fully appreciated the team effort involved in bringing any book to publication. The process of bringing this book to fruition has educated me. I have been extremely fortunate in having the support of a talented and dedicated group of teammates. I cannot voice sufficient accolades for, and express enough gratitude to, Bonny Fetterman for her enthusiasm about this book and the depth of her commitment to it, and for her unrelenting efforts on its behalf which brought it into the good hands of

Ben Yehuda Press. She was a godsend. Thanks, too, to dear friends (many of long standing) who wrote in support of the nascent text: Rabbi Leslie Gutterman, Rabbi James Rudin, Fr. Patrick J. Ryan S.J., Rabbi David Sandmel, Rabbi David Straus, and Rabbi Burton Visotzky. (Of course, its defects cannot be attributed to them. Our friendship softened the book's faults.) I am grateful for your support.

Editing a text can be torturous and laborious. This was not. Laura Logan has been a joy to work with. I thank her and her editing team, including Markham S. Pyle, for their insightful but gentle editing of the book, improving it with each round of editorial oversight. And I offer my gratitude to Larry Yudelson, publisher of Ben Yehuda Press, for his enthusiasm for this book; and voice my admiration for his courage in undertaking to create a Jewish publishing house in the face of many headwinds, bringing this book and other imaginative and important Jewish works to the reading public. Thank you all.

And thank you for reading this book. I hope you find the experience enjoyable and enlightening.

—DFP

# About the Author

Rabbi Daniel Polish has been a congregational rabbi for many years, most recently serving as spiritual leader of Congregation Shir Chadash of the Hudson River Valley in Lagrangeville, New York. Born in Ithaca, New York, he received his B.A. in Philosophy from Northwestern University, was ordained at Hebrew Union College, and earned his Ph.D. in History of Religion from Harvard University.

Throughout the years he has been involved in interfaith dialogue at the highest levels on behalf of the Jewish community. He was part of a team of prominent scholars of religion that met with Muslim religious leaders throughout South Asia for the purpose of promoting interfaith understanding. He participates in ongoing dialogues with the United States Conference of Catholic Bishops and with the National Council of Churches, and served as chair of the International Jewish Commission for Interreligious Consultation (IJCIC), the official interlocutor of the Jewish community with the Vatican and other international religious bodies.

Rabbi Polish is the author of several previous books: *Bringing the Psalms to Life*, *Keeping Faith with the Psalms*, and *Talking About God: Exploring the Meaning of Religious Life with Kierkegaard, Buber, Tillich and Heschel*. He is co-editor of two volumes with Dr. Eugene Fisher: *The Formation of Social Policy in the Catholic and Jewish Traditions* and *Liturgical Foundations of Social Policy in the Catholic and Jewish Traditions*. He serves on the editorial board of *The Journal of Reform Judaism* and of *Current Dialogue*, published by the World Council of Churches. He lives in the Hudson Valley with his wife, Gail Hirschenfang, and has children and grandchildren scattered around the country.

# Reflections on the weekly Torah portion from *Ben Yehuda Press*

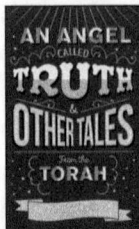

**An Angel Called Truth and Other Tales from the Torah** by Rabbi Jeremy Gordon and Emma Parlons. Funny, engaging micro-tales for each of the portions of the Torah and one for each of the Jewish festivals as well. These tales are told from the perspective of young people who feature in the Biblical narrative, young people who feature in classic Rabbinic commentary on our Biblical narratives and young people just made up for this book.

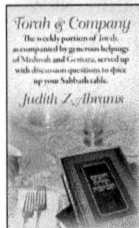

**Torah & Company: The weekly portion of Torah, accompanied by generous helpings of Mishnah and Gemara, served with discussion questions to spice up your Sabbath Table** by Rabbi Judith Z. Abrams. Serve up a rich feast of spiritual discussion from an age-old recipe: One part Torah. Two parts classic Jewish texts. Add conversation. Stir... and enjoy! "A valuable guide for the Shabbat table of every Jew."—Rabbi Burton L. Visotzky, author *Reading the Book*

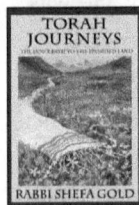

**Torah Journeys: The Inner Path to the Promised Land** by Rabbi Shefa Gold shows us how to find blessing, challenge and the opportunity for spiritual transformation in each portion of Torah. An inspiring guide to exploring the landscape of Scripture... and recognizing that landscape as the story of your life. "Deep study and contemplation went into the writing of this work. Reading her Torah teachings one becomes attuned to the voice of the Shekhinah, the feminine aspect of God which brings needed healing to our wounded world." —Rabbi Zalman Schachter-Shalomi

**American Torah Toons 2: Fifty-Four Illustrated Commentaries** by Lawrence Bush. Deeply personal and provocative artworks responding to each weekly Torah portion. Each two-page spread includes a Torah passage, a paragraph of commentary from both traditional and modern Jewish sources, and a photo-collage that responds to the text with humor, ethical conscience, and both social and self awareness. "What a vexing, funny, offensive, insightful, infuriating, thought-provoking book." —Rabbi David Saperstein

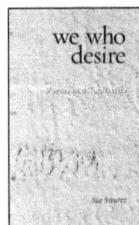

**The Comic Torah: Reimagining the Very Good Book.** Stand-up comic Aaron Freeman and artist Sharon Rosenzweig reimagine the Torah with provocative humor and irreverent reverence in this hilarious, gorgeous, off-beat graphic version of the Bible's first five books! Each weekly portion gets a two-page spread. Like the original, the Comic Torah is not always suitable for children.

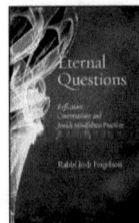

**we who desire: poems and Torah riffs** by Sue Swartz. From Genesis to Deuteronomy, from Bereshit to Zot Haberacha, from Eden to Gaza, from Eve to Emma Goldman, *we who desire* interweaves the mythic and the mundane as it follows the arc of the Torah with carefully chosen words, astute observations, and deep emotion. "Sue Swartz has used a brilliant, fortified, playful, serious, humanely furious moral imagination, and a poet's love of the music of language, to re-tell the saga of the Bible you thought you knew." —Alicia Ostriker, author, *For the Love of God: The Bible as an Open Book*

**Eternal Questions** by Rabbi Josh Feigelson. These essays on the weekly Torah portion guide readers on a journey that weaves together Torah, Talmud, Hasidic masters, and a diverse array of writers, poets, musicians, and thinkers. Each essay includes questions for reflection and suggestions for practices to help turn study into more mindful, intentional living. "This is the wisdom that we always need—but maybe particularly now, more than ever, during these turbulent times." —Rabbi Danya Ruttenberg, author, *On Repentance and Repair*

# Jewish spirituality and thought from *Ben Yehuda Press*

**The Essential Writings of Abraham Isaac Kook.** Translated and edited by Rabbi Ben Zion Bokser. This volume of letters, aphorisms and excerpts from essays and other writings provide a wide-ranging perspective on the thought and writing of Rav Kook. With most selections running two or three pages, readers gain a gentle introduction to one of the great Jewish thinkers of the modern era.

**Ahron's Heart: Essential Prayers, Teachings and Letters of Ahrele Roth, a Hasidic Reformer.** Translated and edited by Rabbi Zalman Schachter-Shalomi and Rabbi Yair Hillel Goelman. For the first time, the writings of one of the 20th century's most important Hasidic thinkers are made available to a non-Hasidic English audience. Rabbi Ahron "Ahrele" Roth (1894-1944) has a great deal to say to sincere spiritual seekers far beyond his own community.

**A Passionate Pacifist: Essential Writings of Aaron Samuel Tamares.** Translated and edited by Rabbi Everett Gendler. Rabbi Aaron Samuel Tamares (1869-1931) addresses the timeless issues of ethics, morality, communal morale, and Judaism in relation to the world at large in these essays and sermons, written in Hebrew between 1904 and 1931. "For those who seek a Torah of compassion and pacifism, a Judaism not tied to 19th century political nationalism, and a vision of Jewish spirituality outside of political thinking this book will be essential." –Rabbi Dr. Alan Brill, author, *Thinking God: The Mysticism of Rabbi Zadok of Lublin*

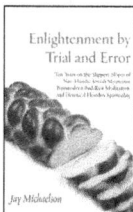

**Return to the Place: The Magic, Meditation, and Mystery of Sefer Yetzirah** by Rabbi Jill Hammer. A translation of and commentary to an ancient Jewish mystical text that transforms it into a contemporary guide for meditative practice. "A tour de force—at once scholarly, whimsical, deeply poetic, and eminently accessible." —Rabbi Tirzah Firestone, author of *The Receiving: Reclaiming Jewish Women's Wisdom*

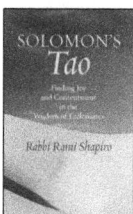

**Enlightenment by Trial and Error: Ten Years on the Slippery Slopes of Jewish Mysticism, Postmodern Buddhist Meditation, and Heretical Flexidox Spirituality** by Rabbi Jay Michaelson. A unique record of the 21st century spiritual search, from the perspective of someone who made plenty of mistakes along the way.

**The Tao of Solomon: Finding Joy and Contentment in the Wisdom of Ecclesiastes** by Rabbi Rami Shapiro. Rabbi Rami Shapiro unravels the golden philosophical threads of wisdom in the book of Ecclesiastes, reweaving the vibrant book of the Bible into a 21st century tapestry. Shapiro honors the roots of the ancient writing, explores the timeless truth that we are merely a drop in the endless river of time, and reveals a path to finding personal and spiritual fulfillment even as we embrace our impermanent place in the universe.

**Embracing Auschwitz: Forging a Vibrant, Life-Affirming Judaism that Takes the Holocaust Seriously** by Rabbi Joshua Hammerman. The Judaism of Sinai and the Judaism of Auschwitz are merging, resulting in new visions of Judaism that are only beginning to take shape. "Should be read by every Jew who cares about Judaism." – Rabbi Dr. Irving "Yitz" Greenberg

# Recent books from *Ben Yehuda Press*

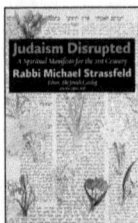

**Judaism Disrupted: A Spiritual Manifesto for the 21st Century** by Rabbi Michael Strassfeld. "I can't remember the last time I felt pulled to underline a book constantly as I was reading it, but *Judaism Disrupted* is exactly that intellectual, spiritual and personal adventure. You will find yourself nodding, wrestling, and hoping to hold on to so many of its ideas and challenges. Rabbi Strassfeld reframes a Torah that demands breakage, reimagination, and ownership." —Abigail Pogrebin, author, *My Jewish Year; 18 Holidays, One Wondering Jew*

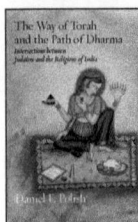

**The Way of Torah and the Path of Dharma: Intersections between Judaism and the Religions of India** by Rabbi Daniel Polish. "A whirlwind religious tourist visit to the diversity of Indian religions: Sikh, Jain, Buddhist, and Hindu, led by an experienced congregational rabbi with much experience in interfaith and in teaching world religions." —Rabbi Alan Brill, author of *Rabbi on the Ganges: A Jewish Hindu-Encounter*

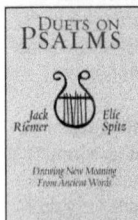

**Liberating Your Passover Seder: An Anthology Beyond The Freedom Seder**. Edited by Rabbi Arthur O. Waskow and Rabbi Phyllis O. Berman. This volume tells the history of the Freedom Seder and retells the origin of subsequent new haggadahs, including those focusing on Jewish-Palestinian reconciliation, environmental concerns, feminist and LGBT struggles, and the Covid-19 pandemic of 2020.

**Duets on Psalms: Drawing New Meaning from Ancient Words** by Rabbis Elie Spitz & Jack Riemer. "Two of Judaism's most inspirational teachers, offer a lifetime of insights on the Bible's most inspired book." — Rabbi Joseph Telushkin, author of *Jewish Literacy* "This illuminating work is a literary journey filled with faith, wisdom, hope, healing, meaning and inspiration." —Rabbi Naomi Levy, author of *Einstein and the Rabbi*

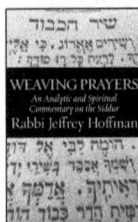

**Weaving Prayer: An Analytical and Spiritual Commentary on the Jewish Prayer Book** by Rabbi Jeffrey Hoffman."This engaging and erudite volume transforms the prayer experience. Not only is it of considerable intellectual interest to learn the history of prayers—how, when, and why they were composed—but this new knowledge will significantly help a person pray with intention (kavvanah). I plan to keep this volume right next to my siddur." —Rabbi Judith Hauptman, author of *Rereading the Rabbis: A Woman's Voice*

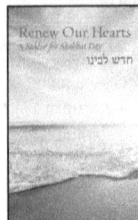

**Renew Our Hearts: A Siddur for Shabbat Day** edited by Rabbi Rachel Barenblat. From the creator of *The Velveteen Rabbi's Haggadah*, a new siddur for the day of Shabbat. *Renew Our Hearts* balances tradition with innovation, featuring liturgy for morning (*Shacharit* and a renewing approach to *Musaf*), the afternoon (*Mincha*), and evening (*Ma'ariv* and *Havdalah*), along with curated works of poetry, art and new liturgies from across the breadth of Jewish spiritual life. Every word of Hebrew is paired with transliteration and with clear, pray-able English translation.

**Forty Arguments for the Sake of Heaven: Why the Most Vital Controversies in Jewish Intellectual History Still Matter** by Rabbi Shmuly Yanklowitz. Hillel vs. Shammai, Ayn Rand vs. Karl Marx, Tamar Ross vs. Judith Plaskow... but also Abraham vs. God, and God vs. the angels! Movements debate each other. Reform versus Orthodoxy, one- two- and zero-state solutions to the Israeli-Palestinian conflict, gun rights versus gun control in the United States. Rabbi Yanklowitz presents difficult and often heated disagreements with fairness and empathy, helping us consider our own truths in a pluralistic Jewish landscape.

# Recent books from *Ben Yehuda Press*

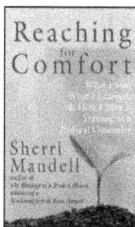

**Reaching for Comfort: What I Saw, What I Learned, and How I Blew it Training as a Pastoral Counselor** by Sherri Mandell. In 2004, Sherri Mandell won the National Jewish Book award for *The Blessing of the Broken Heart*, which told of her grief and initial mourning after her 13-year-old son Koby was brutally murdered. Years later, with her pain still undiminished, Sherri trains to help others as a pioneering pastoral counselor in Israeli hospitals. "What a blessing to witness Mandell's and her patients' resilience!" —Rabbi Dayle Friedman, editor, *Jewish Pastoral Care: A Practical Guide from Traditional and Contemporary Sources*

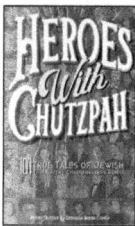

**Heroes with Chutzpah: 101 True Tales of Jewish Trailblazers, Changemakers & Rebels** by Rabbi Deborah Bodin Cohen and Rabbi Kerry Olitzky. Readers ages 8 to 14 will meet Jewish changemakers from the recent past and present, who challenged the status quo in the arts, sciences, social justice, sports and politics, from David Ben-Gurion and Jonas Salk to Sarah Silverman and Douglas Emhoff. "Simply stunning. You would want this book on your coffee table, though the stories will take the express lane to your soul." —Rabbi Jeff Salkin

**Just Jewish: How to Engage Millennials and Build a Vibrant Jewish Future** by Rabbi Dan Horwitz. Drawing on his experience launching The Well, an inclusive Jewish community for young adults in Metro Detroit, Rabbi Horwitz shares proven techniques ready to be adopted by the Jewish world's myriad organizations, touching on everything from branding to fundraising to programmatic approaches to relationship development, and more. "This book will shape the conversation as to how we think about the Jewish future." —Rabbi Elliot Cosgrove, editor, *Jewish Theology in Our Time.*

**Put Your Money Where Your Soul Is: Jewish Wisdom to Transform Your Investments for Good** by Rabbi Jacob Siegel. "An intellectual delight. It offers a cornucopia of good ideas, institutions, and advisers. These can ease the transition for institutions and individuals from pure profit nature investing to deploying one's capital to repair the world, lift up the poor, and aid the needy and vulnerable. The sources alone – ranging from the Bible, Talmud, and codes to contemporary economics and sophisticated financial reporting – are worth the price of admission." –Rabbi Irving "Yitz" Greenberg

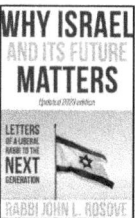

**Why Israel (and its Future) Matters: Letters of a Liberal Rabbi to the Next Generation** by Rabbi John Rosove. Presented in the form of a series of letters to his children, Rabbi Rosove makes the case for Israel — and for liberal American Jewish engagement with the Jewish state. "A must-read!" —Isaac Herzog, President of Israel "This thoughtful and passionate book reminds us that commitment to Israel and to social justice are essential components of a healthy Jewish identity." —Yossi Klein Halevi, author, *Letters to My Palestinian Neighbor*

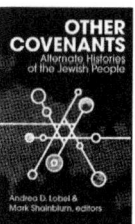

**Other Covenants: Alternate Histories of the Jewish People** by Rabbi Andrea D. Lobel & Mark Shainblum. In *Other Covenants*, you'll meet Israeli astronauts trying to save a doomed space shuttle, a Jewish community's faith challenged by the unstoppable return of their own undead, a Jewish science fiction writer in a world of Zeppelins and magic, an adult Anne Frank, an entire genre of Jewish martial arts movies, a Nazi dystopia where Judaism refuses to die, and many more. Nominated for two Sidewise Awards for Alternate History.